A TABLE FOR SAINT JOSEPH

CELEBRATING MARCH 19TH WITH
DEVOTIONS, AUTHENTIC ITALIAN
RECIPES, AND TIMELESS TRADITIONS

MARY ANNE SCANLAN GRASSO

WestBow
PRESS
A DIVISION OF THOMAS NELSON

WestBow Press books may be ordered through booksellers or by contacting:

WestBow Press
A Division of Thomas Nelson
1663 Liberty Drive
Bloomington, IN 47403
www.westbowpress.com
1 (866) 928-1240

ISBN: 978-1-4908-1647-0 (sc)
ISBN: 978-1-4908-1648-7 (hc)
ISBN: 978-1-4908-1646-3 (e)

Library of Congress Control Number: 2013921405

Printed in the United States of America.

WestBow Press rev. date: 12/13/2013

CONTENTS

DEDICATION PAGE

This book, *A Table for Saint Joseph: Celebrating March 19ᵗʰ with Devotions, Authentic Italian Recipes and Timeless Traditions,* is lovingly dedicated to everyone who has ever worked in any capacity to honor Saint Joseph.

I wish to give thanks and recognition especially to all the members of the Sacred Heart Society of Little York, Houston, Texas—those in the past, present and future for their generous giving of their time, talents and treasures to help the less fortunate in the name of Saint Joseph.

The Sacred Heart Society of Little York was organized in March 1923 by twenty-seven leaders of a small community, in North Houston, known as Little York. These men were all of Italian extraction and of the Roman Catholic faith. They met with Father D. Viola, Pastor of Sacred Heart Catholic Church, in Little York—presently Assumption Catholic Church. They first met in a little barn in back of the little white church. When the church burned to the ground in 1950, they offered the use of their new location to the Pastor. Over the years their charitable donations have not only benefited their own parish but others and their community. The St. Joseph Altar is just one example of their generosity and good will.

IN MEMORIAM

Katie M. Ragusa Porcarello—5 /19/13-10/29/09

Dominic Cuccerre—1/27/30-4/9/11

Rosie Tusa Ragusa—2/7/20-1/22/12

IN GRATITUDE

The writing of this book, *A Table for Saint Joseph: Celebrating March 19th with Devotions, Authentic Italian Recipes and Timeless Traditions,* has been a work of love and enlightenment. I believe that God not only gave me the idea to write this book, but that He has given me insights and wisdom to do so. Thank You, Lord.

Dear Honorable Saint Joseph,

You bless our lives with your shining examples of obedience, faithfulness and love. Thank you for lighting a lamp for our lives to follow the way to Jesus Christ. Amen.

I didn't realize that it not only "takes a village to raise a child", but it takes a multitude of loved ones to help me write a book. This book.

To the love of my life and handsome prince, Johnnie Grasso, who is always at my side and always supportive of me. You light up my life!

My beloved daughter, Judy, opened the door for me to have this book, so dear to my heart, published when all other doors were closed. "Thank you" seems so inadequate when my heart is bursting with joy and appreciation. You can't out give the Lord, my precious angel. And equal thanks go to your wonderful husband, Rich Peplinski. You deserve half the credit, my Rich.

One day, my beloved son, Mike, called and said, "Hi, Mom, what are you doing?" without hesitating, I responded, "Writing a best seller!" And without batting an eye, he said, "Well, I'll buy the first copy!" That's the kind of loving encouragement I've received from all my family and close friends. Thanks to all of you. I can't leave out Mikey's precious two girls: His wife, Yvonne and our youngest granddaughter, Taylor. I love you and appreciate that you're always there for me, too.

I couldn't have done it without my laptop from my generous grandson, Mike Triplett, who drew my name for Christmas. I can hardly wait until he draws my name again! God bless my oldest granddaughter, Beth, and our great-grandchildren, Julia Rose and J.T. for your loving support.

When my inadequate computer skills reduced me to blubbering tears, it was usually my middle granddaughter, Tracy Lynn Peplinski, who rescued me. I couldn't have written this book without her expertise. Thank you for your loving patience with me, my darling girl.

My granddaughter, Rachel Jill Peplinski, your eagerness to search the web for me for referencing information that seemed impossible for me to find, was made possible by you.

My wonderful pastor, Father Charles Samperi, not only gave me and this book a special blessing for its success, but personally wrote a table blessing for a St. Joseph Altar for me and shared a cookie recipe, too. I call that *real* loving support. God bless you, Father!

Our parish's choir director, A. J. Bituin, generously gave me *his* copy of *"We Come to Your Feast"* when he realized that it was a perfect fit for this book. Thank you so much.

And my thanks to Kyle Cothern and GIA Publications, Inc. for permission to include this song in my book.

My dear friend, Sue Wyche, spent many, long hours proofreading my Scriptures and most of my recipes. You are priceless, Sue. And many thanks to my dear friend, Cristy McCallum, and my own Tracy Lynn for proofreading recipes, too. There's a bunch! My sweet granddaughter, Rachel Jill, did a beautiful job on my Bibliography. My daughter, Judy, gave me invaluable insights in editing my Foreword. Another dear friend, Sylvia Szabo, typed all the labels for my many photos. I'm so grateful to all of you.

Many thanks to Anna Marie Pizzitola Allen, my lifetime friend, for allowing me to use her family's recipe book, *Pizzitola Family Cookbook III*. And thanks to Bessie Spedale for sharing the *Ladies of the Sacred Heart Cookbook* with me. Such delicious recipes in both of them. To all who gave me a recipe—many thanks!

To everyone who so graciously shared your own personal stories with me, I am so grateful. Their richness and warmth have enhanced the flavor of this book for all who read it.

I appreciate all the teams at WestBow Press who worked so diligently on my book. I love it! A special thanks to Katherine Montgomery, Megan Leach, Amanda Parsons, Alicia Hewell and Brian Martindale for their special kindness and expertise. God bless yaw'll!

And, to my precious Discalced Carmelite Nuns, of New Caney, Texas, for all your prayers, novenas, encouraging, loving words, I thank you with all my heart. Keep praying for me. Prayer works!

Love and prayers, Mary Anne/Mom/Memaw

FOREWORD

One might well ask me, "Why is a nice, Irish-American, Catholic lady like you writing a book about celebrating a traditionally Sicilian-Italian feast day in honor of Saint Joseph?" Good question. Well, I've been happily married to my wonderful Sicilian-American, Catholic husband, Johnnie Grasso, for over fifty-eight years, now. During this time, I've wholeheartedly embraced many of his ancestors' traditions, customs and foods as my own. One of the traditions that has captured my heart is the Saint Joseph Altar or Saint Joseph Table, as some refer to it. I fell in love with the richness, loving generosity and faithfulness of this feast day celebration the very first time I attended one in the 1950's.

I first experienced a St. Joseph Table as a young bride in March of 1956. One of our cousins, Rosie Tilotta, was offering this Table to petition Saint Joseph's intercession in the healing of her seventeen-year-old son of Leukemia. Rosie felt so helpless in controlling what was happening to her beloved child. This Table enabled her to *do something* for him. The son, Vincent, later died of this dreaded disease. It was so heartbreaking, but I truly believe his mother derived some semblance of peace and acceptance of God's Will knowing she had done all that she could for Vincent by her prayers and by offering this Table in her home. Hosting a Table takes love, time, dedication and a great deal of work. It's a united effort of family and friends to make it all come together successfully.

On the day of Rosie's Table, I recall entering her modest home and delighting in the sights, aromas and sounds surrounding me. In spite of the underlying sadness, there seemed to me to be a sense of joy and expectation in the camaraderie and busyness taking place. The living room's focal point displayed a three-tiered Altar, complete with white altar cloths. It was a thing of beauty—unlike anything I had ever seen. Every available space on each tier held something significant for this occasion. The focal point, a statue of St. Joseph holding Baby Jesus in the center of the top tier, caught my eye. Pies and cakes and cookies with their wonderful aromas tantalized my senses. China plates filled with fried mustard, collard, turnip and other greens made my mouth water in anticipation. Large sculptures made of dough and filled with a fig filling, adorned the Altar. I would later learn the significance of these religious symbols.

The Altar offered fresh fruits and vegetables of all varieties along with vases of fresh flowers. Everything looked so colorful and vibrant and appealing to the eye. Huge loaves of shiny, brown, braided bread stood up against the back of the tiers. I felt a part of something very special and unique. I heard that the priest had already been there to bless the Altar and all the food.

A small bowl of dried beans, unfamiliar to me, displayed a sign to "take one". Aunt Angeline, our "Aunt Glean", encouraged me to take one and keep it in my purse. She said it was a fava bean and considered to be lucky. That if I would always carry one as she did—and she showed me hers—I would never be broke! Well, everyone knew our sweet Aunt Glean *always* had money, so I took one. I reasoned; it couldn't hurt.

Young children, mostly relatives, chosen to be the "saints", were seated at a special table. Once the food had been blessed, they would be served first—a small portion of everything on the Altar, in addition to pasta and sauce, bread and dessert.

The women who had spent weeks preparing for this feast day had prepared huge pots of spaghetti sauce seasoned to perfection. And the men were cooking pasta over an open fire in the backyard in an enormous pot—big enough to feed an army. They would be cooking fresh pasta throughout the day. People would come and go all day to celebrate this special saint's day, partaking of the delicious food while sharing their stories and news with one another. People of all cultures and all backgrounds have a common thread—that of sharing their joys and sorrows while sharing a meal together. Food is the cement that bonds us together with our faith, family and friendships.

That special day at Rosie's Altar, I allowed all the beauty, reverence, congeniality, flavors, and LOVE surround me and fill me up. I vowed I would learn all I could about this special day and perhaps someday write about it. Now, by the grace of God, my dream has come true.

Many believe that Catholics reverence saints in place of God. We do not. We reverence God, The Father, Jesus, Who is God the Son, and the Holy Spirit, Who is also God—making up the Holy Trinity. We do honor saints for the exemplary lives they had led while on earth. We try to emulate them as role models enabling us to live better lives. All of us have been blessed to have had two modern day "saints" such as Pope John Paul II and Mother Teresa of Calcutta to show us the way.

We Catholics do pray directly to our Father and to Jesus. And quite often we pray to a favorite saint to intercede to Them for us. It's like having a favorite friend putting in a good word on one's behalf. Why not? It's worked successfully for ages. In the case of Saint Joseph for example, God, the Father, hand-picked this poor, humble, obedient, honorable, faithful servant to raise His only beloved Son. Why shouldn't we trust in our Father's decision and honor His choice?

During my formative years in El Paso, Texas, my hard-working, disciplinarian father insisted on giving his seven children a Catholic education. The last five of us walked four blocks to St. Joseph's (!) and back home for a simple, but delicious hot lunch every day. My unconditionally-loving mother, a convert to the Catholic faith, encouraged her kids to say the rosary with her and had us sing gospel *and* Latin hymns around her piano. She knew Jesus personally and had a deep devotion to His Blessed Mother, Mary. Actually, all of us were blessed to have had our loving parents who instilled in us a strong faith foundation.

On February 26, 1977, I willfully and consciously made the most important decision of my life. I invited Jesus Christ into my heart as my Lord and Savior. I had known *about* Him all my life. Now I *know* Him personally. We Catholics don't talk much about being "saved" or being "born again", but they're real experiences that do change lives for the better.

On that life-changing day, I attended "A Day of Prayer" with Father Vincent Dwyer at the Rice-Rittenhouse Hotel in downtown Houston, Texas. I will never forget his recurring invitation: "Cut the strings to the world!" This Roman Catholic priest had a new message for all who attended: Repent and confess your sins to God, acknowledge Jesus' dying on the Cross for each one of us sinners and accept His loving forgiveness. Incredible! And, even more incredibly, that Jesus rose from the dead—He's alive! I always knew that in my head. Now, I know it in my heart, too.

The most important verse in the Holy Bible for me is John: Chapter 3, Verse 16:

> Yes, God so loved the world that he gave his only Son,
> that whoever believes in him may not die but may have
> eternal life. (The New American Bible Saint Joseph
> Edition).

I personalize this verse to claim it for my own:

> Yes, God so loved {Mary Anne} that he gave His only
> Son {my Lord and Savior, Jesus Christ, who willingly
> and lovingly suffered and died a horrible death on the
> Cross for my sins and illnesses.}that {if I believe} in him
> {I} may not die but {I} will have eternal life.

Jesus Christ *is* coming again. We Catholics affirm this at Mass every time we recite The Nicene Creed.

There will be a huge celebration at this Wedding Feast. The Church is the Bride. (Revelation 19:5-8 TNAB). The Bridegroom is Jesus Christ coming for His Bride. When the Bridegroom returns, I plan to run out to greet Him with my torch full of oil. (Matthew 25: 1-13 TNAB). I hope that I will see you there, too.

Now, my immediate family has started a tradition several years ago, of getting together and making lots of our Aunt Ruth's fig cookies (cuccidati) for Christmas. (You can't make too many of this family favorite!) My husband was raised with uncles and aunts who loved to get together every Sunday evening. For years, Johnnie and I shared turns hosting these gatherings. Suddenly, we were the older generation! Our children, grandchildren and great-grandchildren have been raised in this wonderful tradition. Today, our children are the hosts. Family get-togethers for any occasion should be filled with laughter, good food and loving memories—regardless of your nationality!

I hope you will be blessed by my efforts to give justice and meaning to the rich tradition, faith and devotion to St. Joseph. I pray that this priceless feast day and its heartfelt devotions, customs and traditions will continue on for countless generations to come.

God bless you and yours, Mary Anne Scanlan Grasso

JOSEPH, MY HERO

"Actions {do} speak louder than words." Case in point—Joseph of Nazareth. Nowhere in Scripture is it recorded that he spoke. No words. Anywhere. Yet, we know him by his actions. Joseph was obedient, honorable and caring. He accepted ridicule and blame for Mary's unwed pregnancy without defense. He obeyed God's instructions immediately. No hesitation. No argument. No question. No wonder God trusted this man, Joseph, with His beloved Son. No wonder.

Only two gospels, Matthew and Luke, give us insights into the man, Joseph. They tell us that in addition to obeying God's Laws, he obeyed the Laws given to Moses by God (Mosaic Law) as well as Roman Law, the law of the land:

> Now this is how the birth of Jesus Christ came about. When his mother Mary was engaged to Joseph, but before they lived together, she was found with child through the power of the Holy Spirit. Joseph her husband, an upright man unwilling to expose her to the law, decided to divorce her quietly. Such was his intention when suddenly the angel of the Lord appeared in a dream and said to him: "Joseph, son of David, have no fear about taking Mary as your wife. It is by the Holy Spirit that she has conceived this child. She is to have a son and you are to name him Jesus because he will save

his people from their sins." All this happened to fulfill what the Lord had said through the prophet:

"The virgin shall be with child and give birth to a son, and they shall call him Emmanuel," a name that means "God is with us." (Isaiah 7:14 TNAB).

When Joseph awoke he did as the angel of the Lord had directed him and received her into his home as his wife. He had no relations with her at any time before she bore a son, whom he named Jesus. (Matthew 1:18-25 TNAB).

Mary was engaged to Joseph: they were living in a state of espousal which usually lasted one year in Galilee. (Matthew 1:18 footnote TNAB).

Mary's immediate response to the Angel Gabriel, upon hearing she had been highly favored and chosen by God to conceive and bear His Son, equaled Joseph's obedience:

In the sixth month {of Elizabeth's pregnancy}, the angel Gabriel was sent from God to a town of Galilee named Nazareth, to a virgin betrothed to a man named Joseph, of the house of David. The virgin's name was Mary.

Upon arriving, the angel said to her: "Rejoice, O highly favored daughter! The Lord is with you. Blessed are you among women". She was deeply troubled by his words, and wondered what his greeting meant. The angel went on to say to her: "Do not fear, Mary. You have found favor with God. You shall conceive and bear a son and give him the name Jesus. Great will be his dignity and he will be called Son of the Most High. The Lord God will give him the throne of David his father. He will rule over the house of Jacob forever and his reign will be without end."

Mary said to the angel, "How can this be since I do not know man?" The angel answered her: "The Holy Spirit will come upon you and the power of the Most High will overshadow you; hence, the holy offspring to be born will be called Son of God. Know that Elizabeth your kinswoman has conceived a son in her old age; she who was thought to be sterile is now in her sixth month, for nothing is impossible with God."

Mary said, "I am the servant of the Lord. Let it be done to me as you say." With that the angel left her. (Luke 1:26-38 TNAB).

"Joseph her husband an upright man unwilling to expose her to the law, decided to divorce her quietly." (Matthew 1:19).

Joseph determined this *before* God's messenger appeared to him in a dream proclaiming that Mary's welcoming womb cradled God's only Son. Joseph undoubtedly *knew* the Mosaic Law about adultery. The fact that he willfully *chose* to do the honorable thing proves his love for Mary. He not only saved Mary from embarrassment, ridicule and condemnation from the neighbors—he saved her life.

"But if this charge is true, and evidence of the girl's virginity is not found, they shall bring the girl to the entrance of her father's house and there her townsmen shall stone her to death, because she committed a crime against Israel by her unchasteness in her father's house. Thus shall you purge the evil from your midst."(Deuteronomy 22:20-21 TNAB).

The second time an angel of the Lord appeared to Joseph in a dream, followed the astrologers' visit. This time his swift obedience saved Jesus' life.

(Matthew 2:13-15 TNAB). After they had left, the angel of the Lord suddenly appeared in a dream to Joseph with the command: "Get up, take the child and his mother, and flee to Egypt. Stay there until I tell you otherwise. Herod is searching for the child to destroy him." Joseph got up and took the child and his mother and left that night for Egypt. He stayed there until the death of Herod, to fulfill what the Lord had said through the prophet:

"Out of Egypt I have called my son." (Hosea 11:1)

(The distance from Bethlehem to Egypt is approximately 300-350 miles.)

(The distance from Egypt to Nazareth is approximately 400 miles.)

Once Herod realized he had been deceived by the astrologers, he became furious. He ordered the massacre of all the boys two years old and under in Bethlehem and its environs, making his calculations on the basis of the date he had learned from the astrologers. What was said through Jeremiah the prophet was then fulfilled:

"A cry was heard at Ramah, sobbing and loud lamentation: Rachel bewailing her children; no comfort for her, since they are no more." (Jeremiah 31:15 TNAB)

The third time recorded that an angel of the Lord appeared to Joseph in a dream took place in Egypt and the fourth time before he and his family settled in Israel:

> (Matthew 2:19-23 TNAB). But after Herod's death, the angel of the Lord appeared in a dream to Joseph in Egypt with the command: "Get up, take the child and his mother, and set out for the land of Israel. Those who had designs on the life of the child are dead." He got up, took the child and his mother, and returned to the land of Israel. He heard, however, that Archelaus had succeeded his father Herod as king of Judea, and he was afraid to go back there. Instead, because of a warning received in a dream, Joseph went to the region of Galilee. There he settled in a town called Nazareth. In this way what was said through the prophets was fulfilled:

> *"He shall be called a Nazorean." Unidentifiable in any Old Testament passage. (Matthew 2:23 footnote TNAB).*

> The next day he {Jesus} wanted to set out for Galilee, but first he came upon Philip. "Follow me," Jesus said to him.

> Now Philip was from Bethsaida, the same town as Andrew and Peter. Philip sought out Nathanael and told him, "We have found the one Moses spoke of in the law—the prophets too—Jesus, son of Joseph, from Nazareth."

> Nathanael's response to that was, "Can anything good come from Nazareth?", and Philip replied, "Come, see for yourself." (John 1:43-46 TNAB).

Jesus, the son of Joseph, a carpenter by trade, worked as a carpenter as was the custom of sons following their fathers' trades in those days:

> He {Jesus} departed from there and returned to his own part of the country followed by his disciples. When the Sabbath came he began to teach in the synagogue in a way that kept his large audience amazed. They said: "Where did he get all this? What kind of wisdom is he endowed with? How is it that such miraculous deeds are accomplished by his hands? Is this not the carpenter, the son of Mary...?" (Mark 6:1-3 TNAB).

In these four instances recorded in Holy Scripture, we observe the willingness and haste with which Joseph responded to God's messenger. In a similar fashion, he responded to the Roman Law of the land when he took Mary, heavy with child, to Bethlehem to be counted in the census. The prophet, Micah, foretold hundreds of years before Jesus' birth that the long-awaited Messiah would be born in Bethlehem:

> But you, Bethlehem-Ephrathah, too small to be among the clans of Judah, From you shall come forth for me one who is to be ruler in Israel; Whose origin is from of old, from ancient times. (Therefore the Lord will give them up, until the time when she who is to give birth has borne, And the rest of his brethren shall return to the children of Israel.) He shall stand firm and shepherd his flock by the strength of the Lord, in the majestic name of the Lord, his God; And they shall remain, for now his greatness shall reach to the ends of the earth; he shall be peace. (Micah 5:1-3).

I call it one of God's Coincidences (God's Master Plan) that Caesar Augustus, the Roman ruler, ordered the *very first census ever taken* at the *exact* time of the birth of Jesus Christ. This authentic record establishes Joseph as the father of Jesus.

Bethlehem, a small village, is located just under 100 miles from Nazareth.

> In those days Caesar Augustus published a decree ordering a census of the whole world. This first census took place while Quirinius was governor of Syria. Everyone went to register, each to his own town. And so Joseph went from the town of Nazareth in Galilee to Judea, to David's town of Bethlehem—because he was of the house and lineage of David—to register with Mary, his espoused wife, who was with child. While they were there the days of her confinement were completed. She gave birth to her first-born son and wrapped him in swaddling clothes and laid him in a manger, because there was no room for them in the place where travelers lodged. (Luke 2:1-7 TNAB).

Years ago, a nurse friend of mine, Mrs. Pat Buchanan, Director of Birthright North in Houston, Texas, told me something I consider profound. She believed that Mary's visit to her kinswoman, Elizabeth, who was six months pregnant with John the Baptist, was part of God's Plan, too. In an important, significant way: to instruct Mary with the birth of her own baby, Jesus. Only God, the Father, would know that Mary and Joseph, a young, inexperienced couple, would be alone, without help, at His birth. Alone in a place where animals fed. Although Scripture does not confirm this, it's reasonable to assume that Mary having stayed three months with Elizabeth, would *not* have gone home just prior to John's birth. Sounds like another God's Coincidence to me. God thinks of everything! (I can just picture John doing cart wheels and summersaults in Elizabeth's womb knowing his Savior was in Mary's womb! Can you see it?)

Angel Gabriel's words to Mary concerning Elizabeth:

"…Know that Elizabeth your kinswoman has conceived a son in her old age; she who was thought to be sterile is now in her sixth month, for nothing is impossible with God."

Mary said: "I am the servant of the Lord. Let it be done to me as you say." With that the angel left her.

Thereupon Mary set out, proceeding in haste into the hill country to a town of Judah, where she entered Zechariah's house and greeted Elizabeth.

When Elizabeth heard Mary's greeting, the baby leapt in her womb. Elizabeth was filled with the Holy Spirit and cried out in a loud voice: "Blest are you among women and blest is the fruit of your womb. But who am I that the mother of my Lord should come to me? The moment that your greeting sounded in my ears, the baby leapt in my womb for joy. Blest is she who trusted that the Lord's words to her would be fulfilled."

Then Mary said: "My being proclaims the greatness of the Lord, my spirit finds joy in God my savior, For he has looked upon his servant in her lowliness; all ages to come shall call me blessed. God who is mighty has done great things for me, holy is his name; His mercy is from age to age on those who fear him. He has shown might with his arm; he has confused the proud in their inmost thoughts. He has deposed the mighty from their thrones and raised the lowly to high places. The hungry he has given every good thing, while the rich he has sent empty away. He has upheld Israel his servant, ever mindful of his mercy; Even as he promised our fathers, promised Abraham and his descendants forever."

Mary remained with Elizabeth about three months and then returned home. (Luke 1:36-56 TNAB).

It is obvious that Joseph remained at Mary's side during the birth of Jesus. When the heavenly host of angels appeared to the shepherds in the fields proclaiming the birth of the Messiah and Lord, they hastened to find Jesus, just as they had been told:

> There were shepherds in that locality, living in the fields and keeping night watch by turns over their flocks. The angel of the Lord appeared to them as the glory of the Lord shone around them, and they were very much afraid. The angel said to them: "You have nothing to fear! I come to proclaim good news to you—tidings of great joy to be shared by the whole people. This day in David's city a savior has been born to you, the Messiah and Lord. Let this be a sign to you: in a manger you will find an infant wrapped in swaddling clothes."
>
> Suddenly, there was with the angel a multitude of the heavenly host, praising God and saying,
>
> "Glory to God in high heaven, peace on earth to those on whom his favor rests."
>
> When the angels had returned to heaven, the shepherds said to one another: "Let us go over to Bethlehem and see this event which the Lord has made known to us." They went in haste and found Mary and Joseph, and the baby lying in the manger; once they saw, they understood what had been told them concerning this

child. All who heard of it were astonished at the report given them by the shepherds. (Luke 2:8-18 TNAB).

Imagine a God—so loving and personal—that He came down to earth in the form of a helpless baby dependent upon His very existence on Mary and Joseph. Imagine that! He could have been born in a palace with servants and all the luxuries, but instead chose to be born in poverty so that He could identify with us and we could identify with Him. Amazing! He could have chosen any man on earth to raise Him. And He chose Joseph—evidently a man after His own heart—as was David, the shepherd boy turned king, Joseph's ancestor. God's plans are always perfect. God rejected all seven of David's brothers before choosing David to be anointed by Samuel, a prophet of God:

> … But the Lord said to Samuel: "Do not judge from his appearance or from his lofty stature, because I have rejected him. Not as man sees does God see, because man sees the appearance but the Lord looks into the heart." (Samuel 16:7 TNAB).

> …Then Samuel asked Jesse {David's father}, "Are these all the sons you have?" Jesse replied, "There is still the youngest, who is tending the sheep." Samuel said to Jesse, "Send for him; we will not begin the sacrificial banquet until he arrives here." Jesse sent and had the young man brought to them. He was ruddy, a youth handsome to behold and making a splendid appearance. The Lord said, "There—anoint him, for this is he!"

> Then Samuel, with the horn of oil in hand, anointed him in the midst of his brothers; and from that day on, the spirit of the Lord rushed upon David…. (Samuel 16: 11-13 TNAB)

Joseph proved his obedience to Mosaic Law (first given to Abraham by God) by circumcising (most probably doing it himself) Jesus eight days after his birth:

> God also said to Abraham: "On your part, you and your descendants after you must keep my covenant throughout the ages. This is my covenant with you and your descendants after you that you must keep: every male among you shall be circumcised. Circumcise the flesh of your foreskin, and that shall be the mark of the covenant between you and me. Throughout the ages, every male among you, when he is eight days old, shall be circumcised...." (Genesis 17:9-12 TNAB)

God's part of this covenant with Abraham (formerly Abram) promised a multitude of descendants if Abraham would walk blameless in His presence:

> When Abram was ninety-nine years old, the Lord appeared to him and said: "I am God the Almighty. Walk in my presence and be blameless. Between you and me I will establish my covenant, and I will multiply you exceedingly." (Genesis 17:1-2 TNAB).

Joseph followed the Mosaic Law, given to Moses by God, when he presented Jesus to God in the Temple at Jerusalem. **Jerusalem is about five miles south of Bethlehem.** This took place at the same time as Mary's purification which required a sacrifice in keeping with their income. Their sacrifice of two young pigeons or a pair of turtledoves indicate they were not wealthy although Joseph descended from royalty:

> When the day came to purify them according to the law of Moses, the couple brought him up to Jerusalem so that he could be presented to the Lord, for it is written

in the law of the Lord, "Every first-born male shall be consecrated to the Lord." They came to offer in sacrifice "a pair of turtledoves or two young pigeons," in accord with the dictate in the law of the Lord. (Luke 2:22-24 TNAB).

According to Mary's purification stated in the Law of Moses:

The Lord said to Moses, "Tell the Israelites: When a woman has conceived and gives birth to a boy, she shall be unclean for seven days, with the same uncleanness as at her menstrual period. On the eighth day, the flesh of the boy's foreskin shall be circumcised, and then she shall spend thirty-three days more in becoming purified of her blood; she shall not touch anything sacred nor enter the sanctuary till the days of her purification are fulfilled. If she gives birth to a girl, for fourteen days she shall be as unclean as at her menstruation, after which she shall spend sixty-six days in becoming purified of her blood. When the days of her purification for a son or for a daughter are fulfilled, she shall bring to the priest at the entrance of the meeting tent a yearling lamb for a holocaust and a pigeon or a turtledove for a sin offering. The priest shall offer them up to the Lord to make atonement for her, and thus she will be clean again after her flow of blood. Such is the law for the woman who gives birth to a boy or a girl child. If, however, she cannot afford a lamb, she may take two turtledoves or two pigeons, the one for a holocaust and the other for a sin offering. The priest shall make atonement for her, and thus she will again be clean." (Leviticus 12:1-8 TNAB).

The last time we "see" Joseph in Scriptures is when Jesus is twelve-years-old and The Holy Family travels to Jerusalem, with others, to celebrate Passover. This observance has also been in obedience to what God instructed Moses in Egypt:

> Moses called all the elders of Israel and said to them, "Go and procure lambs for your families, and slaughter them as Passover victims. Then take a bunch of hyssop, and dipping it in the blood that is in the basin, sprinkle the lintel and the two doorposts with this blood. But none of you shall go outdoors until morning. For the Lord will go by, striking down the Egyptians. Seeing the blood on the lintel and the two doorposts, the Lord will pass over that door and not let the destroyer come into your houses to strike you down.

> You shall observe this as a perpetual ordinance for yourselves and your descendants. Thus, you must also observe this rite when you have entered the land which the Lord will give you as he promised. When your children ask you, 'What does this rite of yours mean?' you shall reply, 'This is the Passover sacrifice of the Lord, who passed over the houses of the Israelites in Egypt; when he struck down the Egyptians, he spared our houses.' "

> Then the people bowed down in worship, and the Israelites went and did as the Lord had commanded Moses and Aaron. (Exodus 12: 21-28 TNAB)

Joseph proved to be an excellent role model for his Son (and for us) to follow by his examples in complete obedience to God's Laws and man's laws. He also exemplified his love, protection, concern, honor and faithfulness in his care of Mary and Jesus in all of his actions. Mary speaks for Joseph and for herself when they find their lost son in the temple after frantically searching for him:

> His parents used to go every year to Jerusalem for the feast of the Passover, and when he was twelve, they went up for the celebration as was their custom. As they were returning at the end of the feast, the child Jesus remained behind unknown to his parents. Thinking he was in the party, they continued their journey for a day, looking for him among their relatives and acquaintances.
>
> Not finding him, they returned to Jerusalem in search of him. On the third day they came upon him in the temple sitting in the midst of the teachers, listening to them and asking them questions. All who heard him were amazed at his intelligence and his answers.
>
> When his parents saw him they were astonished, and his mother said to him: "Son, why have you done this to us? You see that your father and I have been searching for you in sorrow." He said to them: "Why did you search for me? Did you not know that I had to be in my Father's house?" But they did not grasp what he said to them.
>
> He went down with them then, and came to Nazareth, and was obedient to them. His mother meanwhile kept all these things in memory. Jesus, for his part, progressed steadily in wisdom and age and grace before God and men.
>
> (Luke 2:41-52 TNAB)

We do not know when or how Joseph died. We do not see him in any of the Gospel accounts of Jesus' Passion and Death. John, who refers to himself as "the beloved apostle", records how he and Mary, Jesus' grieving mother, stood at the foot of the Cross. When Jesus' dying instructions to John were to care for His mother, we are led to believe that Joseph is no longer living to take care of her:

> Near the cross of Jesus there stood his mother, his mother's sister, Mary the wife of Clopas, and Mary Magdalene. Seeing his mother there with the disciple whom he loved, Jesus said to his mother, "Woman, there is your son." In turn he said to the disciple, "There is your mother." From that hour onward, the disciple took her into his care. (John 19:25-27 TNAB).

Just as The Catholic Church has assumed Mary, Jesus' Blessed Mother, into Heaven, so might we assume this faithful servant of God, Joseph, earthly father of Jesus, into Heaven, also. This beautiful Scripture, reflection and prayer sum up our sentiments:

> Scripture. Standing near the Cross of Jesus were His mother and His mother's sister, Mary the wife of Clopas, and Mary Magdalene. (John 19:25).

Patron of the Dying

Reflection. At his death Jesus was surrounded by people who loved Him. The Bible does not reveal what happened when Joseph died. He simply disappeared from the Scriptures after the incident of finding Jesus in the temple.

It seems reasonable to believe that Joseph died in the arms of Mary and Jesus. The Church accordingly lists him as the Patron of the Dying.

Prayer. Dear St. Joseph, bring your calm presence to me at the moment of my death. (Day by Day with St. Joseph).

HONORS AND DEVOTIONS

According to **The New Catholic Encyclopedia**, it took the Catholic Church many years to grant Saint Joseph the recognition and honor he deserved:

St. Joseph

…. Only under the pontificate of Sixtus IV (1471-84), were the efforts of these holy men rewarded by the introduction of the feast of St. Joseph into the Roman Calendar (March 19). From that time the devotion acquired greater and greater popularity, the dignity of the feast keeping pace with this steady growth. …Benedict XIII, in 1726, inserted the name into the Litany of the Saints.

One festival in the year, however, was not deemed enough to satisfy the piety of the people. The feast of the Espousals of the Blessed Virgin and St. Joseph, so strenuously advocated by Gerson, and permitted first by Paul III to the Franciscans, then to other religious orders and individual dioceses, was, in 1725, granted to all countries that solicited it, a proper Office, compiled by the Dominican Pietro Aurato, being assigned, and the day appointed being January 23. Nor was this all, for the reformed Order of Carmelites, into which St. Teresa had infused her great devotion to the foster-father of Jesus, chose him, in 1621, for their patron, and in 1689, were allowed to celebrate the feast of his patronage on the third Sunday after Easter. This feast, soon adopted throughout the Spanish kingdom, was later on extended to all states and dioceses which asked for the privilege. No devotion, perhaps, has grown so universal, none seems to have appealed so forcibly to the heart of the Christian people, and particularly of the laboring classes, during the nineteenth century, as that of St. Joseph.

CHARLES L. SOUVAY

Removed from "http//oce.catholic.com/index.php?

title=Joseph%2CSaint

Copyright @ 1979-2008 Catholic Answers

In **The Dictionary of the Saints**, Second Edition, John J. Delaney adds to the honors bestowed upon the earthly father of Jesus the Christ

Joseph (1st century). …. Special veneration to Joseph began in the East, where the apocryphal *History of Joseph* enjoyed great popularity in the fourth to the seventh centuries. In the West, the ninth-century Irish *Felire* of Oengus mentions a commemoration, but it was not until the fifteenth century that veneration of Joseph in the West became widespread, when his feast was introduced into the Roman calendar in 1479; his devotion was particularly popularized by St. Teresa and St. Francis de Sales. Joseph was declared Patron of the Universal Church by Pope Pius IX in 1870; a model for fathers of families by Pope Leo XIII, who confirmed that his preeminent sanctity places him next to the Blessed Virgin among the saints, in his encyclical *Quamquam pluries in 1889;* a protector of workingmen by Pope Benedict XV; the patron of social justice by Pope Pius XI; and in 1955, Pope Pius XII established the feast of St. Joseph the Worker on May 1.

Sermon 2, On Joseph
By St. Bernardine of Siena

"This is the general rule that applies to all individual graces given to a rational creature. Whenever divine grace selects someone to receive a particular grace, or some especially favoured position, all the gifts for his state are given to that person, and enrich him abundantly.

This is especially true of that holy man Joseph, the supposed father of our Lord Jesus Christ, and true husband of the queen of the world and of the angels. He was chosen by the eternal Father to be the faithful foster-parent and guardian of the most precious treasures of God, his Son and his spouse. This was the task which he so faithfully carried out. For this, the Lord said to him, 'Good and faithful servant, enter into the joy of your Lord.'

A comparison can be made between Joseph and the whole Church of Christ. Joseph was the specially chosen man through whom and under whom Christ entered the world fittingly and in an appropriate way. So, if the whole Church is in the debt of the Virgin Mary, since, through her, it was able to receive the Christ, surely after her, it also owes to Joseph special thanks and veneration.

For he it is who marks the closing of the old testament. In him the dignity of the prophets and patriarchs achieves its promised fulfillment. Moreover; he alone possessed in the flesh what God in his goodness promised to them over and over.

It is beyond doubt that Christ did not deny to Joseph in heaven that intimacy, respect, and high honour which he showed to him as to a father during his own human life, but rather completed and perfected it. Justifiably the words of the Lord should be applied to him. 'Enter into the joy of your Lord.' Although it is the joy of eternal happiness that comes into the heart of man, the Lord prefers to say to him 'enter into joy'. The mystical implication is that this joy is not just inside man, but surrounds him everywhere and absorbs him, as if he were plunged in an infinite abyss.

Therefore be mindful of us, blessed Joseph, and intercede for us with Him Whom men thought to be your Son. Win for us the favour of the most Blessed Virgin your spouse, the mother of Him Who lives and reigns with the Holy Spirit through ages unending. Amen."

(http.//www.fisheaters.com/customslent5html) **5/14/07**

And from **Blessed Josemaria Escriva:**

"St. Joseph was an ordinary sort of man on whom God relied to do great things. He did exactly what the Lord wanted him to do, in each and every event that went to make up his life."

http://www.bulin.com/stjoe/sjlife.html 3/19/2004

The following **Litany of Saint Joseph and Prayer** are taken from **Day by Day with St. Joseph**, a daily devotional, published in 2010 in celebration of 100 years of publishing by The Catholic Publishing Corporation. (Devotions by Msgr. Joseph Champlin and Msgr. Kenneth Lasch. New Jersey Copyright 2010)

Litany of St. Joseph

Lord, have mercy.	Joseph, most Faithful,
Christ, have mercy.	*pray for us.*
Lord, have mercy.	Mirror of Patience,
Christ, hear us.	*pray for us.*
Christ, graciously hear us.	Lover of Poverty
God, the Father of heaven,	*pray for us.*
have mercy on us.	Model of Artisans,
God the Son, Redeemer of the world,	*pray for us.*
	Glory of Home Life,
have mercy on us.	*pray for us.*
God the Holy Spirit,	Guardian of Virgins,
have mercy on us.	*pray for us.*
Holy Trinity, one God,	Pillar of Families,
have mercy on us.	*pray for us.*
Holy Mary, *pray for us.*	Solace of the Wretched,
St. Joseph, *pray for us.*	*pray for us.*
Renowned offspring of David,	Hope of the Sick,
pray for us.	*pray for us.*
Light of Patriarchs,	Patron of the Dying,
pray for us.	*pray for us.*
Spouse of the Mother of God,	{Patron of the Unborn,
pray for us.	*pray for us.}*
Chaste guardian of the Virgin,	Terror of Demons,
pray for us.	*pray for us.*
Foster Father of the Son of God,	Protector of Holy Church,
pray for us.	*pray for us.*

Diligent Protector of Christ, *pray for us.*	Lamb of God, You take away the sins of the world; *spare us, O Lord!*
Head of the Holy Family, *pray for us.*	Lamb of God, You take away the sins of the world; *graciously hear us, O Lord!*
Joseph most Just, *pray for us.*	
Joseph most Chaste, *pray for us.*	Lamb of God, You take away the sins of the world; *have mercy on us.*
Joseph most Prudent, *pray for us.*	V. He has made him the lord of His household.
Joseph most Strong, *pray for us.*	
Joseph most Obedient, *pray for us.*	R. And Prince over all His possessions.

Prayer

Let us pray. O God, in Your ineffable providence You were pleased to choose Blessed Joseph to be the spouse of Your most Holy Mother. Grant, we beg You, that we may be worthy to have him for our intercessor in heaven whom on earth we venerate as our Protector: You who live and reign forever and ever. Amen.

The New Catholic Encyclopedia sheds more light on Jesus' right to be called the "Son of David":

JOSEPH, ST.

LIFE. In Mt. 1. 6—16, where Joseph's father is called Jacob, his ancestry is traced back to King David through the latter's son Solomon; but in Lk 3.23—32, where Joseph's father is called Heli, his ancestry is traced back to David through the latter's son Nathan. The two lines of descent are thus completely different, except for their convergence at Salathiel and Zorobabel (Mt 1.12; Lk 3.27). The obvious purpose of both lists is to show that Jesus, by being the legal son of Joseph, had a right to be called the "Son of David" (Mt 15.23), a recognized title of the Messiah (Mt 22—42).

In regards to the idea that Joseph was an old man at the time of Christ's birth:

...Art and imagination have usually pictured Joseph as an old man. But this is surely a false idea. The rabbis at the time of Christ commonly taught that men should marry between the ages of 13 and 19, and Joseph as a "just" (i.e., law-abiding) man, would no doubt have conformed to this practice.

To clarify the Virgin Birth and the Catholic Church's view on it:

...The Evangelist, however, immediately warns the reader that he (Joseph) did not consummate the marriage: "He did not know her till she brought forth her first-born son." The only purpose of the latter statement is to insist that Mary was a virgin at the birth of Jesus. It says nothing, one way or the other, regarding the relations between Joseph and Mary after the birth of Jesus. The Catholic doctrine of the perpetual virginity is based on tradition that goes back to the earliest age of the Church.

JOSEPH, ST., DEVOTION TO

Patronage and Feast

...The feast of St. Joseph the Worker on May 1 was promulgated by Pius XII in 1955.... The choice of May 1 was made to counteract atheistic communism's celebration of May Day, and to emphasize the dignity of labor, Christian ideals in labor relations, and the example of St. Joseph as a workman. The Feast of the Holy Family (on the first Sunday after Epiphany) commemorates the hidden life that Jesus shared with Mary and Joseph. In that sense it is a feast of St. Joseph. Ever since 1815, petitions have been sent to the Holy See from hundreds of bishops and thousands of layfolk asking for the inclusion of St. Joseph's name in the *Confiteor, Suscipe Sancta Trinitas, Communicantes,* and *Libera Nos Quaesumus* of the Mass. The inclusion would be a means of granting him an honor more proportioned to his dignity as head of the Holy Family and Patron of the Universal Church, for he would be recognized as such in the liturgy. By a decree of John XXIII dated Nov. 13, 1962, and effective Dec. 8 of the same year, the name of St. Joseph was finally inserted into the *Communicantes.*

The precious **Discalced Carmelite Nuns of New Caney, Texas** have been giving me so much encouragement and praying for the success of this book. They have also graciously given me permission to include this novena in it.

Novena in Honor of St. Joseph

Novena in honor of St. Joseph composed by the Discalced Carmelite Nuns of San Antonio, Texas. Reflection texts for each day taken from Pope John Paul II's Encyclical on St. Joseph, "Redemptor Custos." (No date or copyright listed)

Prayer for each day

Heavenly Father, You gave St. Joseph a share in Your fatherhood and placed him as a father to Jesus on earth. Help us to be obedient to Your will as he was. Teach us the way of prayer that we may enjoy the friendship of Mary and Jesus as did St. Joseph. During life's hardships, give us courage to walk with those who need us that we may be enriched by their gifts. Carry us through sufferings and trials with St. Joseph at our side. (pause to pray for your intentions) And may we look to him at the final hour of death. We ask this through Your Son, Jesus. Amen.

DAY ONE

Reflection: Inspired by the Gospel, the Fathers of the Church from the earliest centuries stressed that just as St. Joseph took loving care of Mary and gladly dedicated himself to Jesus Christ's upbringing, he likewise watches over and protects Christ's Mystical Body, that is, the Church, of which the Virgin Mary is the exemplar and model.

The whole Christian people not only turn to St. Joseph with great fervor and invoke his patronage with trust, but also keep before their eyes his humble, mature way of serving and of "taking part" in the plan of salvation.

Prayer for each day:

DAY TWO

Reflection: Joseph took Mary in all the mystery of her motherhood. He took her together with the Son who had come into the world by the power of the Holy Spirit. In this way he showed a readiness of will like Mary's with regard to what God asked of him through the angel.

Prayer for each day:

DAY THREE

Reflection: Together with Mary, Joseph shares in the final phase of God's self- revelation in Christ. Looking at the gospel texts of both Matthew and Luke, one can also say that Joseph is the first to share in the faith of the Mother of God, and that in doing so he supports his spouse. He is also the first to be placed by God on the path of Mary's "pilgrimage of faith."

Prayer for each day:

DAY FOUR

Reflection: Joseph's fatherhood—a relationship that places him as close as possible to Christ, to whom every election and predestination is ordered (cf. Rom 8:28-29)—comes to pass through marriage to Mary, that is, through the family.

The Savior began the work of salvation by the virginal and holy union, wherein is manifested his all-powerful will to purify and sanctify the family—that sanctuary of love and cradle of life.

Prayer for each day:

DAY FIVE

Reflection: St. Joseph was called by God to serve the person and mission of Jesus. His fatherhood is expressed concretely "in his having made his life a service, a sacrifice to the mystery of the Incarnation and to the redemptive mission connected with it ....

Joseph showed Jesus "by a special gift from heaven, all the natural love, all the affectionate solicitude that a father's heart can know."

Prayer for each day:

DAY SIX

Reflection: Journeying to Bethlehem for the census in obedience to the orders of legitimate authority, Joseph fulfilled for the child the significant task of officially inserting the name, "Jesus, son of Joseph of Nazareth" (cf. Jn 1:45) in the registry of the Roman Empire. This registration clearly shows that Jesus belongs to the human race as a citizen of this world, subject to laws and civil institutions, but also "savior of the world."

Prayer for each day:

DAY SEVEN

Reflection: Now when (the magi) had departed, behold, an angel of the Lord appeared to Joseph in a dream and said, "Rise, take the child and his mother, and flee to Egypt, and remain there till I tell you; for Herod is about to search for the child, to destroy him" (Mt 2:13). Joseph, "took the child and his mother by night, and departed to Egypt, and remained there until the death of Herod."

Just as Israel had followed the path of the exodus in order to begin the Old Covenant, so Joseph, even in exile watched over the one who brings about the New Covenant.

Prayer for each day:

DAY EIGHT

Reflection: Within the surroundings of the Holy Family of Nazareth, Jesus "grew and became strong, filled with wisdom; and the favor of God was upon him." (Lk 2:40). Only one episode from this "hidden time" is described in the Gospel of Luke: the Passover in Jerusalem when Jesus was twelve years old. Together with Mary and Joseph, Jesus took part in the feast as a young pilgrim. "And when the feast was ended, as they were returning, the boy Jesus stayed behind in Jerusalem. His parents did not know it." (Lk 2:43). After a day's journey, they noticed his absence and began to search among their kinsfolk and acquaintances. "After three days they found him in the temple, sitting among the teachers, listening to them and asking them questions; and all who heard him were amazed at his understanding and his answers" (Lk 2:47). Mary asked: "Son, why have you treated us so? Behold, your father and I have been looking for you anxiously" (Lk 2:48). The answer Jesus gave was "How is it that you sought me? Did you not know that I must be in my Father's house?" (Lk 2:49-50) Joseph, of whom Mary had just used the words "your father," heard this answer. The reply of Jesus in the Temple brought once again to his mind that he was a guardian of the mystery of God.

Prayer for each day

DAY NINE

Reflection: The total sacrifice, whereby Joseph surrendered his whole existence to the demands of the Messiah's coming into his home, becomes understandable only in the light of his profound interior life. It was from this interior life that "very singular commands and consolations came, bringing him also the logic and strength—giving him the power of making great decisions—such as the decision to put his liberty at the disposition of divine designs.

Besides trusting in Joseph's sure protection, the Church also trusts in his noble example, which transcends all individual states of life and serves as a model for the entire Christian community, whatever the condition and duties of each of its members may be.

Prayer for each day

A prayer to St. Joseph, the Worker, from Pope Pius IX:

"Glorious St. Joseph, model of all who are devoted to labor, obtain for me the grace to work in the spirit of penance in expiation of my many sins; to work conscientiously by placing love of duty above my inclinations; to gratefully and joyously deem it an honor to employ and to develop by labor the gifts I have received from God, to work methodically, peacefully, and in moderation and patience, without ever shrinking from it through weariness or difficulty to work; above all, with purity of intention and unselfishness, having unceasingly before my eyes death and the account I have to render of time lost, talents unused, good not done, and vain complacency in success, so baneful to the work of God. All for Jesus, all for Mary, all to imitate thee, O patriarch St. Joseph! This shall be my motto for life and eternity."—
Pope Pius IX

To St. Joseph for Protection

"Gracious St. Joseph, protect me and my family from all evil as you did the Holy Family. Kindly keep us ever united in the love of Christ, ever fervent in the imitation of the virtue of our Blessed Lady, your sinless spouse, and always faithful in devotion to you. Amen."—**From the Franciscan Mission Associates**

From Catholic Online

"Saint Joseph, patron of the universal Church, watch over the Church as carefully as you watched over Jesus; help protect it and guide it as you did with your adopted son. Amen."

From The American Prayer Book

May 1. Saint Joseph the Worker Prayer: "Joseph, unlike Jesus and Mary, you were just like us. You were not God's only begotten Son, and yet you were created to raise and protect and guide in human ways, God's Son. You were not born without sin, and yet you were created to be husband to a woman born without sin. In theory, then, you were just like us, and yet, how often can we say we are just like you, and diligent workers. Guide us to do the labor God gives us, in our families and in our workplaces, without complaints or self-pity. Strengthen us with the patience to accept our lot in life and follow the path God has set us on. Amen.

From *Echoes,* Dominican Nuns, Farmington Hills, Michigan

St. Joseph-The Silent Saint

"One of our sisters recently remarked that her favorite invocation for St. Joseph, and one she dearly wished would be added to the Litany of

St. Joseph is: 'Keeper of the Secret.' How appropriate for the dear foster father of Jesus and the spouse of Mary!"

Saint Joseph Table Blessing

(This blessing was specially written for this book by my beloved pastor, **Father Charles Samperi**, St. James the Apostle, Spring, Texas.)

Good and humble St. Joseph,
God chose you to be the provider and protector of Jesus and Mary.
You said yes to God
to His plan of salvation.
You knew the life of the poor as you
journeyed to Bethlehem, not knowing where to lay your head,
but trusting in God's generosity.
You fled to Egypt to protect the Son of God
as soldiers were dispatched to take his life.
At Nazareth, you provided for them by the sweat of your brow and
the work of your hands as a carpenter.
You watched over them with
love and care,
provided for their needs.
And when your last breath was drawn,
they stood by your side with honor and grace.

Give us the grace to welcome all
as we would welcome the Holy Family.
Give us the strength to be humble,
always following God's call.
May we, like you,
be trusting in the path that God has for us.
May we be uncomplaining and filled with
love for God and one another.

St Joseph, look down on this humble table
and ask God to bless it.
May all who come here and share in this meal,
be welcomed and treasured.
May they find the nourishment that is needed,
in order that they have the physical strength
to do the work of God.
May they encounter and know God's love
as they partake in this meal.
We ask all these things
in the name of Jesus Christ our Lord
Amen.

The Ritual Blessing in Sicilian

From the Internet

St. Joseph holds up two fingers of Jesus' right hand.
St. Joseph says and Jesus repeats (3 times):

Benedette la Cena
Benedette Maddalena
Benedette tutte quando.
Patri, Figli, e Spiritu Santu
Quando, Quando, Che Angele Sante.
Patri, Fligli, Spiritu Santu.

(Bless this meal, Bless Maddalena, Bless everyone, Father, Son and Holy
Spirit. When, when, what Sainted Angels. Father, Son and Holy Spirit.)

PERSONAL STORIES

In January 2009, I made a promise to myself to help others prepare for a Saint Joseph Table, and to attend as many Tables as possible. (I attended five!) Every Sunday morning, from 9:00-12:00, for six weeks prior to March 19th, Saint Joseph's feast day, I assisted in making Italian cookies. I joined the senior members of the Sacred Heart Society of Little York (A community located in the North part of Houston, Texas) in this endeavor. This benevolent organization began in 1923. Many people refer to their location as The Sacred Heart Hall, but actually it is The Whitney Oaks Hall. I will never forget the wonderful memories of my experiences with these precious people. I enjoyed every minute of it!

I felt acceptance, gratitude and warmth from all the members—even though I'm mostly Irish! As we say here in Texas, "I claim kin" to being part Sicilian after being married to Johnnie all these years. Four of the married couples at the Hall are distant cousins of my husband. I suspect that if you put six Italians in a room, three will be related by blood, and three by marriage! This is a good thing.

Every year for the past twenty years, approximately thirty members have come faithfully to The Sacred Heart Society Hall for this important event. They're predominately Americans of Sicilian-Italian heritage. Many are married couples, some widowed. Most are middle-aged or older. Some are younger. All appeared enthusiastic and eager to work.

One of my favorites, Katie Porcarello, a youthful ninety-five-year-old, delighted me with her sharp mind and quick wit. When I told her that I'd love to have known her when she was young—that I'll bet she was a "hoot", she looked around and asked others, "What's a hoot?" When they laughingly explained, she grinned and replied, "Girl, I was trouble!" (I learned much later that Katie was Jake Ragusa's sister. And since Jake is married to my husband's cousin, Katie and I are practically kin!)

Most of the ladies at the hall, dress up in attractive dress pants and blouses, wearing jewelry and makeup. This is a social event. They wear aprons and plastic gloves while sitting at oblong tables. These tables have been covered with white butcher paper that has been taped to the edges. Armed with paring knives and small rolling pins made from dowel sticks, the women socialize and patiently wait for the cookie dough to be brought to them. They will shape the dough into the designated cookie of the day. I helped to shape these traditional Italian cookies: sesame seed, fig- filled (cuccidati), biscotti, wedding ring, and pignollati (pine cones). Each person has her own cookie sheet lined with parchment paper. When the cookie sheets are filled, someone will pick them up and place them in the huge commercial ovens. It's a team effort. Everyone knows his/ her job and performs it willingly. There's a lot of camaraderie taking place around these tables and also in the kitchen. I witnessed joy and pleasure in everyone's participation.

Working in the adjoining kitchen are the men—mixing, baking, and later on sacking the finished products in zip lock type baggies. Five-gallon plastic containers with airtight lids and plastic liners store these cookies that will be sold on the day of the Table. It's a tremendous effort, but work shared makes it enjoyable. It's a labor of love for a most worthy cause—feeding the poor. (More on that later on.)

A young man, Damian Palermo, probably in his early thirties, brought his young son, maybe eight, into the kitchen one day. They stood at a stainless steel table across from me. The father lovingly, patiently directed every step in the process of shaping a fig-filled cookie (cuccidati) to his son. Then he allowed the boy to shape them by himself. Imparting this knowledge in such a loving manner that this precious tradition will be passed on to the next generation. I could see the joy they shared in this experience. (It brought tears to my eyes then, and now, each time I read this.)

***

Sam and Bessie Spedale, married for sixty-one years in 2009, organized the very first church Altar in 1965 in Houston, Texas at St. Theresa Catholic Church. Until then, Altars had been held mostly in private homes. For the first two or three years, they drew a tremendous crowd. Then, others began organizing Altars in their own parishes, and the crowd dwindled. So they stopped having them. Later on, in 1989, Sam and Bessie, in cooperation with Oscar Porcarello, organized the first Altar for the Sacred Heart Society of Little York.

Twenty years ago, they started out with a very small Altar which has grown larger and more elaborate each year. In addition to selling cookies and fresh baked bread and items from the Altar after the feast, the members serve a delicious pasta dinner to a large crowd. Before the meal is served, a Catholic priest blesses the Altar, all the food, *and* the workers before serving Mass in the Hall. This is typical of this feast day celebration.

Any undertaking of this magnitude calls for a strong leader to keep everything running smoothly. Bessie Spedale orchestrates, what I call, this "Symphony of Love". She knows how things should be done and efficiently explains the procedures. This woman can get things accomplished; I greatly admire her leadership skills. I loved the way she set up her little statue of Saint Joseph in the kitchen asking his blessing on our day. Every day ran smoothly and effectively as everyone worked good-naturedly together.

***

Bessie Spedale was named after her father, Benjamin Russo's, mother, Viagio—Bessie, in Italian—who remained in Corleone, Sicily. In 1906, Bessie's mother, Frances and *her* best friend from childhood, Bessie Petronella, sailed to America from their home in Corleone, in the Palermo Province of Sicily. Their ship, the Vincenzo Florio Robatino docked at New Orleans, Louisiana. Finally, in April 1963, these best friends who had lived on the same street and gone to the same school as children and who had remained best friends for almost seventy-five years finally realized a dream fulfilled. Two of their grandchildren were united in Holy Matrimony—making them family!

Bessie Spedale's earliest memories of St. Joseph Altars began at age eight. She and her mother walked to Lee Dimicelli's grocery store near their home. There, Bessie would help her mother and other ladies make cookies for the Altar. She just loved it.

She remembers years ago when she counted thirteen different kinds of cooked vegetables on the Altar. These were small quantities cooked specifically for the "saints", the little children chosen to sit at a special table. It was customary for each "saint" to have a small taste of each blessed, cooked food item from the Altar in addition to a plate of pasta, bread and goodies. The Sacred Heart Society Hall does not have the traditional "saints' as part of their celebration. Some organizations and churches do, but it is not as common anymore.

Bessie recalls her mother having Altars in their home as she grew up. She portrayed a "saint" many times. As a teenager she remembers the custom of attending <u>nine</u> Altars in one day, making a Novena to Saint Joseph. Bessie reminisces, "When I was a teen, everyone knew who would be hosting an Altar in their home. One year, my friends and I started out in the late afternoon to make this Novena. It was late at night when we arrived at the last house and the family had already gone to bed. We woke the people up! I told them 'Look, this is our <u>ninth</u> Altar for our Novena. You've <u>got</u> to let us in to see your Altar and say a prayer.' And they did!"

One time Bessie's mother had 12 old men sit at the "saints" table instead of the twelve children usually designated. Sam Spedale remembers going to that Altar as a teenager, but doesn't remember meeting Bessie until later on.

***

Sam and Bessie Spedale have happy faces with eyes that sparkle and light up reflecting their love of life and willingness to serve others. They love what they are doing—and have spent their lifetimes of working to feed the poor.

Sam smiled throughout my interview with him. It's as though he had joy bubbling up inside. He confided to me that the pronunciation of his last name has been Americanized. It should be Spe-doll-ee, but he answers to Spee-dale. He noticed signs along the streets in Rome with Spedale on them. He discovered it translated to Hospital!

Sam had a mother and grandmother who had numerous Altars in their homes when he was growing up. They would go to others and beg for items for the Altar. Begging is a tradition of having or "doing" an Altar. Some people would give money. Every nickel received would be spent on food and later given away along with the items left on the Altar. He said they would fix bags of the blessed food from the Altars and give them to the minorities and whites alike who needed them. When I asked him if he had ever been chosen as a "saint", he immediately responded with a big laugh, "Never! And I'm still not a saint."

He grew up in a small town called High Bank near Bryan, Texas. He remembers in those days there were no tables or chairs to eat your feast day meal. Everyone would sit on the hood or trunk of somebody's car and enjoy their plate of pasta. No one cared!

When Sam returned from serving in the army during World War II, his father had moved to Houston. A buddy invited Sam to go to a wedding and afterwards to The Plantation Restaurant on South Main Street in Houston. Sam said, "I don't know anybody there." His friend responded, "You know me!" And that's where he met Bessie. I asked him if he liked her right away and he said, "Not really." Then, he changed the subject and told me how much Bessie loved sports. "I have to sit 2 or 3 seats away from her at games because she'll beat me up when she gets so excited!" Sam must have taken a second look at Bessie and liked what he saw; they were married February 1, 1948. They have a son and a daughter, 5 grandchildren and 12 greats! Sam and Bessie Spedale are special role models for all of us to follow. God bless them!

All of the expenses weren't in yet for the 2009 Altar at the Hall—but the year before they netted over three thousand dollars! That's a lot of pasta dinners and cookies, etc. sold. With that money, the members bought non-perishable food items and hams and filled one-hundred boxes. This has been their tradition over the years. They donated 5 boxes to 20 various churches to be distributed to the less-fortunate. What a glorious ministry—Saint Joseph would be proud!

***

Archbishop Emeritus, for the Galveston-Houston Archdiocese, Joseph A. Fiorenza shared his memories with me:

"The special devotion given to St. Joseph on his name's day was a traditional practice from my earliest childhood.

Several families erected altars in honor of our saint and invited children to represent Mary and Joseph and many of the saints. I vividly recall being one of the saints for a couple of years in the home of a relative. The parish church also had a large beautiful altar prepared and invited parishioners to pray to our great saint and protector.

Both children and adults always looked forward to March 19 to offer special prayers to St. Joseph at altars which were true works of art in their beauty, adorned with specialty baked bread and delicious Italian cookies, beautiful flowers amidst a statue of Mary, Joseph and the Christ Child. Besides offering devotion to St. Joseph for his protection, the altars were a reminder to provide food for the poor to honor St. Joseph, the Father of the Poor.

The food from the altar and the donations received were designated to help the poor. I hope the St. Joseph Altar devotion will continue to have a special place in the customs of future generations of Italian-Americans."

***

Our cousins and charter members of the Sacred Heart Society, Jake and Rosie Ragusa, shared their delightful story with me in October 2011. He was 92 and Rosie 91. They had been married 70 years! They raised 4 children and lost one to cancer. Now, they are enjoying their 8 grandchildren and 4 greats! When I called their home for this interview, Jake informed me he was cooking some pasta for their dinner and enjoying a glass of wine while preparing the meal laughing delightedly, as usual. When I asked Rosie if she had been a "saint" as a child, she said, "Yes, five or six times." I could hear Jake from the kitchen saying, "Twelve times!" Later on, he would be helping Rosie from her wheelchair into bed. Both of them so congenial and helpful in telling me their story. They seemed inseparable to me. I'd never seen one without the other—forever sweethearts.

Jake and Rosie first met in 1941 at a dance held at Assumption Catholic Church in Little York. The old church hall, that later burned down, held dances on weekends—a popular place for young people. Rosie told me Jake's brother, Nathan, introduced them. When I asked her how long she had known Nathan she replied, "About five minutes!" She chuckled and admitted to introducing herself to Nathan so that *he* would introduce her to Jake. She had her eye on Jake! They danced together and liked each other right away. It was a type of square dance music where someone blew a whistle and everyone changed partners. They were married on June 1, 1941 and *never* again changed partners!

After they married, they took over Jake's parents' grocery store. Then, on February 12, 1942, Jake received his draft notice from Uncle Sam. When he went into the army, Jake's sister, Rosie Tamborello, bought the store from him. Upon his discharge in December 1945, Rosie sold the store back to Jake because of her husband's poor health.

One of the wonderful memories Jake experienced when he returned from World War II was a complete surprise to him. His wife's cousin, Frances Rizzo, held a Saint Joseph's Altar in her home in March 1946. She invited 13 servicemen, in different branches of the military, to sit at her "saints" table in their uniforms! She wanted to honor these young men for fighting and risking their lives for our country's freedom. She wanted to give thanks to God and to Saint Joseph for their safe return. (Our cousin, Catherine Ciulla, portrayed Mary.)

Jake Ragusa and our own Uncle Pete Frenza, and Oscar Porcarello, three of these honored guests, were overwhelmed by the experience. This was a celebration of thanksgiving. So many prayers to God and St. Joseph were answered when these young men returned home safely. No more tears. No more sadness. No more worry. Only joy and laughter. Home at last! Safe and sound!

***

My wonderful pastor, Father Charles Samperi, of Saint James the Apostle Catholic Church in Spring, Texas, recalled his memories: He was *never* chosen to be a "saint"—being too mischievous as a boy. His family owned a bakery here in Houston in the early 1960's. They sold Italian bread to restaurants. Every year, prior to March 19th, his father would close up their bakery for a special event. Several old Italian ladies would spend one long day baking huge loaves of Panne Grosse (big bread) and fig cookies (cuccidati) for their Saint Joseph Altars. The tantalizing aromas would waft throughout the bakery. Little Charlie couldn't understand one word of their friendly chatter, but he certainly understood the smiling faces offering him large pieces of hot bread loaded with butter to his heart's delight.

Another special memory of Father Charles took place in the 1980's at St. Christopher Catholic Church in SE Houston. About 25 parishioners, including himself, were busy cleaning the entire church—top to bottom—dusting the stations of the cross—and all. This in preparation for their Saint Joseph Altar. A generous-hearted, anonymous gentleman overheard someone say they needed a statue of Saint Joseph to make their Altar complete. In no time at all, a four feet statue of the saint, shipped all the way from New York, arrived just in time for the feast day!

***

Another cousin, George Zuckero, president of the men's Sacred Heart Society, remembers being chosen as a "saint" twice. The first time he was very young, and portrayed Saint Joseph for his Aunt Katie Perrone's Altar. And the second time for his Aunt Mary Ciulla. He doesn't recall the saints' names… He does remember that the "saints' were given a small portion of everything on the Altar. And they had to eat every bite of the blessed food served to them. George says that when he was about ten-years-old, he watched men cooking large quantities of pasta in a garage for an Altar. They were using a brand new #3 washtub and a big boat paddle to stir the pasta. He was in awe of this sight.

***

Once, our longtime dear friend, Richard Allen, helped his father-in-law, Tannie Guy Pizzitola, cook pasta in a new #3 washtub, too. He had a bonfire in the backyard for Mrs. Pizzitola's Altar. At the end of a long, arduous day, Richard had about thirty pounds of cooked pasta left over. When he asked his father-in-law if he should just throw it away, Mr. P. told him to just throw it over the fence to his goat. Regrettably, the goat ate *all* thirty pounds of pasta, swelled up and died!

***

Floyd "Bubba" Miller takes charge of the large commercial mixer at the Sacred Heart Society Hall. In addition to making the dough for the cookies, he bakes round loaves of bread for the sale. He attended his first Altar 25 or 26 years ago at his uncle and aunt's—Oscar and Pauline Porcarello. In years past, he's made the large, braided loaves of Panne Grosse for the Sacred Heart Society's Altar. Now, they order those from a bakery. And "Bubba" makes the smaller round loaves to sell on the feast day. He planned to bake 60 or 70 loaves for this Altar. When I asked him if he had ever been chosen as a "saint" he grinned and replied, "No, I was *never* a saint." I asked him if he had ever prayed for something specific from Saint Joseph. He said, "That everyone has work. I remember a priest, in Chicago years ago, saying, 'How dare you pray for anything. Just thank God for what you have.' " A lesson for all to learn.

***

Lillian Lena Musachia Emmite Pizzitola, always smiling, always joking. Every time I saw her at the Hall, she'd smile at me and say "I'm Lillian". Such a loving personality. Everyone seems to love her. When I asked several members who had made that most delicious sauce I had ever eaten, (for the feast day dinner) the unanimous answer I got—Lillian! This is a "meatless feast", (since traditionally, this feast day falls during Lent) so, the sauce has to be seasoned well to be flavorful. Lillian told me that the men had made 40 gallons of sauce to which she added anchovies, sardines, fresh fennel and "other good things", that she buys, to make it outstandingly, uniquely delicious. (See Lillian's Melanese Sauce in the Recipe section).

Lillian said, "With all the trauma in my life, I donate my time and work here. The people here are so loving. I have twin sons, Fred and Tom, who are grown. Fred had cancer in the kidneys and colon. Now, he's healed! Now, Tom has a brain tumor. My donation of time and work for Saint Joseph is for him to get well."

That interview took place in March 2009. Today is March 6, 2012. I phoned Lillian today for an update. The first question I asked her was about Tom's condition. He's healed, too!

She corrected the diagnosis for Tom. It wasn't a brain tumor, but a blister on the back of his skull and many, many blood clots on his lungs. All of these things dissolved on their own! Sounds like answered prayer to me! And Lillian agreed. I asked her if she had prayed to Saint Joseph for Fred's healing, too. She said she not only prayed to him but also to the Blessed Mother to talk to her Son! What an awesome testimony.

***

Johanna Traina Petronella, another friendly member of the Sacred Heart Society, shared with me how her grandmother, Frances Gagliano, in Corleone, Sicily, knew when it was time to come to the Altar. Someone would light a huge bonfire to alert everyone. It could be seen for miles around. This annual event was a big occasion to celebrate for everyone.

***

In the past, Rose Ann Leonetti has been president of The Charity Guild of St. Joseph for three terms. This organization is part of the ICC— Italian Cultural Center. It is part of The Federation which includes a number of other groups made up of Catholic women.

"After my mother, Vita Sedita Leonetti, passed away in 1996, I wanted to get involved with the Charity Guild of St. Joseph. My mother was devoted to St. Joseph. She helped with Altars when I was growing up. She made the big sculptures with inedible bread and fig filling that decorate the Altars so beautifully for Holy Family Catholic Church in Missouri City, Texas, a suburb of Houston.

She also helped with The Charity Guild before she died. I just wanted to continue what she had started. I've been blessed and I want to give back to people less fortunate.

My mother helped with Altars when I was growing up. My father was ill with diabetes and she offered these Altars for his recovery. He did get better. And I've had prayers to St. Joseph, for myself, answered, too. St. Joseph has helped me a lot. I've been a "saint" 4 or 5 times as a small child. My grandchildren have been "saints" at Altars, too. I want them to realize this rich heritage and to continue it.

Many years ago, before my time as president, Guild members would find a number of homeless people on the streets to be the "saints' at their Altar. They would get them clothes and transportation to and from the feast. They did this for many years.

Now, The Charity Guild of St. Joseph sends out newsletters to members and businesses for donations for their St. Joseph Altar. They "beg" for food donations and baked items to sell from restaurants, also. Every donation they receive gives them that much more profit to donate to the poor. They average between $10,000 and $12,000 profit each year. They donate at least $10,000 to St. Vincent de Paul to distribute to the poor each year, among other charities."

Rose Ann is still a member of The Guild. As she said before, "I've been blessed and I want to give back to people less fortunate."

***

I met three precious sisters who shared their stories with me over the phone. These are sisters by blood—not nuns—but they surely could have been nuns by their loving generosity. Their names are Frances Pollizzio, Vita Rossi and Dorothy Piazza.

Frances Pollizzio, born April 17, 1921, at ninety-one-years *young*, in 2012, is <u>still</u> creating large, beautiful sculptures for St. Joseph Altars for the Sacred Heart Society and private homes! And without charge! This lovely lady says it takes an average of 2 hours or more to fashion one of these unique, inspirational pieces of art. She starts in the middle of January every year to make them for the Sacred Heart Society.

"I like to take my time. I don't follow a pattern. I feel The Holy Spirit inspires me to do these. Once, another lady and I were to make 20 sculptures. By the middle of February she had only made four! I prayed to St. Joseph and did the rest of them myself.

The dough determines the way it will go. I make edible dough for the big sculptures, also. But it's not soft like the little ones (cuccidate). I handle dough more for sculptures and it's a stiffer dough.

My mother's name was Mary Ferreri. I was raised in the Houston area—Alief, Texas. When I was eleven-years-old, I had double pneumonia and was severely ill. On Christmas Eve night, a young man, named Frank Bova, came to our door. He had come to go hunting with my father. But when he realized how ill I was, he talked my father into taking me to the hospital. My father took me to St. Joseph's Hospital in Houston. A priest came and gave me last rites (for the dying). All of my mother's friends were there praying for me. Doctor Crapitto gave me a shot of a new experimental drug called penicillin. That's what helped me! I opened my eyes and said, 'I'm here!' I think it brought me closer to God. In thanksgiving, my mother had an Altar to St. Joseph. I still believe that young man was an angel sent by God.

Before I went to the hospital, I was so sick. Something came to me. I don't know what. I went into a tunnel. I saw such beautiful people walking around—sleep walking. Someone asked me, 'Would you like to stay here?' I said, 'No!' Then I came awake. It wasn't my time, perhaps. Perhaps I was meant to live and make these sculptures. I love making them."

And, dear, sweet Frances, may I say, "Everyone is blessed to see your beautiful works of art. Thank you for sharing your God-given talents so generously with all of us who are privileged to see them."

***

Vita Rossi, 86, never had a St. Joseph's Altar in her home for the homeless, but she organized the very first Altar for them at the Magnificat House in Houston, Texas, taught them arts and crafts and has continued to volunteer there for twenty-two years!

"My parents, Vito and Mary Ferreri, always believed in St. Joseph. My mother taught me and my sisters how to make fig cookies when we were little. We had Altars in our home growing up.

I believe it was 1990 when I was invited to a Christmas party given by the Teresian Fifth Dimension Club. This club is named after St. Teresa of Liseaux, France. These Catholic women vow to *do more* for people less fortunate than themselves. They accept the Teresian style of living which includes these five dimensions: Spirituality, Education, Vocation, Community and Ministry. When everyone got old and sick, this chapter finally folded after twenty years of exceptional service to others. I've never seen any other group of women do such beautiful work. They took care of the Magnificat House.

The Christmas party was held at the Magnicat House. The residents there were former mental patients of the State Hospital in Austin,

Texas. Once they were able to take their own medication, they were put on buses and sent back to their hometowns. They had no families and no place to go. Most of them were rescued from living under the underpasses in downtown Houston. These residents are free to come and go outside. They usually take a short walk not too far, and they can leave whenever they wish or they can remain for life—*if* they obey the rules.

I had an urge to do something, Mary Anne; you know how it is? It explodes in you. I didn't like to clean house anymore. My doctor told me to quit cleaning toilets and get involved with something. I kept having these feelings of helping and doing for others.

On Holy Thursday that year, my son and I went to the Magnificat House. Bishop John Morkovsky came to wash the residents' feet {as Christ washed His Apostles' feet at the Last Supper}. Residents wore mismatched clothes that were donated to them. Psychiatrists gave speeches listing the needs of these people. An Art Dept. was one of their needs. I had been involved with art before this. As my son, Andrew, about 27, drove home, I asked him what he thought of me teaching art to the residents. He responded, 'Don't you see they need you?' I thought to myself, *How do I know if I know what to do.*

It seemed there were so many signs helping me to decide. When I went to Mass, the priest told everyone 'You are talented and you must share your talents with the less fortunate or else your talents will be taken away.' Everywhere I went I kept hearing that. I'm riding down the road and I become aware that every telephone pole is in the form of a cross and that told me I had to go forward.

When my fine, young hairdresser, Angelo, whom I dearly loved, heard what I kept thinking about doing, he looked shocked for a moment. He had taught art to homeless people in California before moving here. And, he was willing and eager to help me! We started an Arts and Crafts program once a week for three hours each session at the Magnificat House. I attended an Art class myself at that time. I told my teacher and class what I was doing and that I needed some supplies donated. I told my class 'I need paints and brushes—if you don't donate them, I'm going to steal them from you!' They said, 'Here, here' and gave me their supplies. Before long, people were sending me money and I was able to buy more supplies.

On a field trip to Austin State Hospital with my fellow Teresians, I saw that everything they were doing in their Art Dept. I had been doing. I was doing it right!

One day, I began thinking that the residents at Magnificat House didn't even know about St. Joseph or his feast day. So, I decided to have an Altar for them. Ross Greco, a member of the Sacred Heart Society, made 3-tiered Altars out of wood for anyone and everyone. And he made one for me. He put rollers on it so that it could be moved easily from room to room. I asked him for volunteers to help with the feast day meal. Sacred Heart Society members came to cook and serve 150 residents pasta, hard boiled eggs and all the extras. At home, I made150 bags of St. Joseph cookies, myself. We used paper plates and paper cups, but I bought metal forks and linens. Someone donated flowers for the Altar. It was so beautiful. For our first Altar we had the residents as our "saints". I had the Altar there for five years.

Some of the volunteers were afraid of the residents, not knowing their backgrounds. I've spent 22 years at Magnificat House and I've never had one incident in all that time. They know the rules and they follow them. And, they appreciate everything we do for them.

About three years ago, my sister, Dorothy, and I went to the Magnificat House on St. Joseph's feast day to share lunch with them, again. They still had the Altar set up year round in the dining room with the big loaves of dried bread and sculptures. There were artificial fruits and flowers.

No one bothered any of it. All the food that had been donated that day was peanut butter and jelly and bread. So, we celebrated St. Joseph's Day with the residents eating peanut butter and jelly sandwiches.

In the 1980's, a woman named Rosemary Badami owned 2 shotgun houses near downtown Houston. She and a nun, Sister Kathy, lived in those shotgun houses. {A shotgun house is a narrow, rectangular house with rooms one right behind the other and a door at each end.} Together they would search out the homeless: men, women, young women with children, under bridges, highways, byways, etc. and offer them a home and nourishment. The demand got bigger and bigger. People began donating houses for them to use for the homeless. Restaurants and grocery stores began donating food. Others began sending in money. Eventually it grew into 150 houses for the homeless!

Rosemary Badami, the founder of Magnificat House in Houston, grew up in Victoria, Texas. She witnessed her Italian mother cook big meals and going out to find and invite homeless people into her home. She would seat them at her fine table with linens, china and crystal. Rosemary couldn't understand, as a child, why her mother would invite these odd-looking strangers into their home. But, years later, she not only understood, but she emulated her mother's Christ-like example. "For whatever you do for the least of my brothers, you do unto Me."

After five years of doing the Altar and Art classes, I got tired. Some of the other older volunteers did, too. I have one son, Andrew and two daughters, Tina and Mary Ann. They never complained about my volunteering. I still went every week to help out in other areas, but I didn't teach classes anymore. And, then the nuns from Guatemala came to take over for us!"

**

The third sister, Dorothy Piazza, 83, also a Teresian, is a member of the Charity Guild of St. Joseph:

"The Guild is 100 years old. My parents were some of the original founders. The members still have St. Joseph Altars every year held at St. Theresa's Catholic Church in the Memorial area of Houston, Texas. We donate an average of ten thousand dollars annually to The Food Bank of the City of Houston. The Guild donated twelve thousand dollars to them in 2011 from Altar proceeds and personal donations. The Food Bank tells us that by our giving them cash they can buy three times the amount of food for the entire city than we can. This Food Bank was started about ten years ago by Mary Keegan and Sister Frances Klinger.

My husband died young and I had five children to raise, so I didn't get as involved as my sisters. I did help Vita teach art classes some. The residents at Magnificat House loved the art classes. They had mental problems and whatever they had going on in their minds that day is what they would paint.

I still make the large sculpture pieces for Altars. Also, Vita and I teach classes in making these sculptures. We even have some men who come to classes. They remember their mothers used to make them when they were young and they want to learn how to make them, too.

A few years ago, a priest from Mexico came to a St. Joseph Altar. He was so impressed with the sculptures. He said he wanted to take this knowledge back to his country and teach the women there how to make them. He told us 'This is a gift from God—I want to bless all of your hands.' And he did.

Any homeless person can walk into any Catholic Church and he/she can get a ten dollar check made out to the nearest grocery store. I saw this with my own eyes.

Yes, I was a "saint" for an Altar, one time. My granddaughters remember being "saints", too. They know they got a special grace for that. My whole family has been involved volunteering at the Fishes and Loaves Soup Kitchen on Congress Street in Houston. Our parents taught us well. It's something of value that we can pass down to our families, hopefully for all families, for generations to come."

***

My precious sister-in law, Rosalie Grasso Macejewski, told me that she and my husband, Johnnie, were chosen on numerous occasions to be "saints". Usually, they were invited separately to different Altars hosted by their cousins. This was a very special occasion for them. She remembers vividly how they were each given a big loaf of Saint Joseph's bread and a bag of cookies from the Altar to take home. They so looked forward to attending this event each year. One year, both children contacted chicken pox at the time of the feast day. They were devastated! They would have to wait another long year in hopes of being invited again.

***

Johnnie and Rosalie's maternal grandfather, Giovanni Fiorenza/John Frenza, celebrated his eightieth birthday on our wedding day with his eight children proudly standing next to him in a photo. Everyone loved this sweet, kind, gentle man. He probably didn't weigh much more than one hundred pounds with all of his clothes on, but he worked hard most of his life. Grandpa Frenza emigrated from St. Christine Village in Gela County, a province of Palermo, Sicily when he was about 17 in 1892 to New Orleans, Louisiana. He found work in the sugar cane fields in St. Charles Parish. He met and married Rosalie Cosimano there. While in Louisiana, Grandma gave birth to the first of their eight children, my mother-in-law, Madeline.

Not long after that, they moved to Houston, Texas and bought 12 acres of farm land in the North part of town called Little York. Some folks kindly referred to it as "Little Italy" since so many Italian farmers lived there.

Grandpa Frenza's entire family helped raise produce when they became old enough. He drove his horse-drawn wagon, full of his crops, to The Farmers' Market located near downtown Houston, close to the Santa Fe Train Depot, during the 30's and 40's. His family's livelihood depended solely on the sale of his produce until his children became old enough to work for wages.

On a rare occasion, after selling all of his crops and when he had a dime to spare, Grandpa would treat himself to a movie downtown. Then he would come home and gather all his family around him and retell the entire movie to his captive audience. They loved it! It was <u>almost</u> as good as being there.

Grandma Rosalie Frenza worked hard raising eight children in a small framed house with no running water. Every drop of water had to be pumped from an outdoor well and hauled indoors and boiled for everything: cooking, cleaning, laundry, bathing. Imagine that! She never knew the luxury of owning her own indoor bathroom. This hard life was typical for most of the people she knew, so she accepted it without complaint.

Grandma baked 12 loaves of homemade bread in an outdoor oven at least once a week. She cooked big, filling meals, mostly from the crops they raised. Meat was a luxury. They raised one hog a year and made good use of everything but the oink! She canned jars of vegetables and fruits to carry them through the winter months, and made clothes for her family, often out of the material from feed sacks.

Grandma Frenza, like many women in those days, was the spiritual leader of the family. She attended Mass and made Novenas to her favorite saints. Her children and grandchildren received their sacraments and were taught to love God, Country and Family.

I'm so sorry I didn't get to meet Grandma Frenza. She died of diabetes in 1947, before I met Johnnie. She helped Mama Grasso raise Johnnie and Rosalie. I'd just like to thank her for doing such a good job. I'm truly blessed to be a part of this wonderful family.

Family is a big deal with most Italians, I've discovered. They enjoy getting together and talking and eating. Find an Italian who *doesn't* enjoy good company and a good meal—show me! As I said before, I'm part Sicilian after 58 years, and I love these wonderful times together with loved ones. We're loud and everyone's talking at once and eating way too much—but it's so delicious and the laughter! Life is so good! God is good—all the time.

Now, my immediate family has started a tradition several years ago, of getting together and making lots of our Aunt Ruth's fig cookies (cuccidati) for Christmas. (You can't make too many of this family favorite!) My husband was raised with uncles and aunts who loved to get together every Sunday evening. For years, Johnnie and I shared turns hosting these gatherings. Suddenly, we were the older generation! Our children, grandchildren and great-grandchildren have been raised in this wonderful tradition. Today, our children are the hosts. Family get-togethers for any occasion should be filled with laughter, good food and loving memories—regardless of your nationality!

St. Joseph's Altar "saints" Feast- When Mr. and Mrs. D.V. Rizzo honored
the Feast of St. Joseph, they invited returned veterans to dine with them
in their home at 708 Archer. Feasters are, left to right, S.-Sgt Oscar
Porcarello, Sgt. Charles Giamalva, S.-Sgt Tony Orlando, S-Sgt. Jake
Ragusa, Miss Catherine Ciulla, Cpl. Frank Gusemano, Sgt. Lee Scalise,
S 1-c A.M. Polker, Merchant Seaman 3-c Leon Campise, S 2-c Gasper
Geacone Jr., Cpl. Joe Bruscia, Pfc. Nash Tilotta, and Cpl. Pete Frenza
(our handsome Uncle) is front right with a big smile, March 1946.

Sam & Bessie Spedale-
Co-founders of St. Joseph Altar at Sacred Heart Hall, 1989
Sacred Heart Society Hall, Houston, Texas
Photo Taken by Mary Anne Scanlan Grasso, March 2009

Floyd "Bubba" Miller & Angelo Cassaro with
Sam Spedale (background) mixing dough for Italian Cookies
Sacred Heart Society Hall, Houston, Texas
Photo Taken by Mary Anne Scanlan Grasso - March 2009

St. Joseph Altar/Table
Sacred Heart Society Hall, Houston, Texas
Photo Taken by Mary Anne Scanlan Grasso, March 2012

HEART- Sacred Heart of Jesus and Immaculate Heart of Mary
CHALICE- Chalice of Christ with Grapes- Vineyards of Sicily
PANNE GROSSE- Big Bread
Sacred Heart Society Hall, Houston, Texas
Photo Taken by Mary Anne Scanlan Grasso, March 2012

Lamb of God Cake- Jesus, The Lamb of God
Sacred Heart Society Hall, Houston, Texas
Photo Taken by Mary Anne Scanlan Grasso, March 2009

Panne Grosse (Big Bread)- Star of Bethlehem
Sacred Heart Society Hall, Houston, Texas
Photo Taken by Mary Anne Scanlan Grasso, March 2009

Monstrance- Holds the Sacred Host
Lamb of God cake- Jesus, the Lamb of God
Cross with Dove- Crucifixion of Christ
Dove- The Holy Spirit
Sheaves of Wheat- Abundance of the Earth
Wine- The Miracle at Cana & Jesus' Blood.
St. Ignatius Loyola Catholic Church, Spring, Texas
Photo Taken by Mary Anne Scanlan Grasso, March 2009

Heart- The Sacred Heart of Jesus and the Immaculate Heart of Mary
PUPACULOVA- Baked bread filled with dyed Easter
eggs symbolizing the coming of Easter.
St. Ignatius Loyola Catholic Church, Spring, Texas
Photo Taken by Mary Anne Scanlan Grasso, March 2009

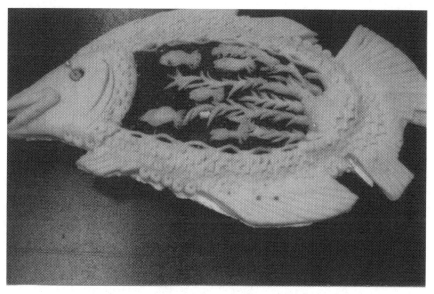

FISH- Christian symbol of Jesus and Christianity
Sacred Heart Society Hall, Houston, Texas
Photo taken by Mary Anne Scanlan Grasso, March 2009

STAFF- St. Joseph's Staff
CHALICE OF CHRIST- with grapes- Vineyards of Sicily
Sacred Heart Society Hall, Houston, Texas
Photo taken by Mary Anne Scanlan Grasso, March 2009

Sandals represent the feet of Jesus, Mary & Joseph
Basket with flowers represents Spring/New Life
Sacred Heart Society Hall, Houston, Texas
Photo taken by Mary Anne Scanlan Grasso, March 2009

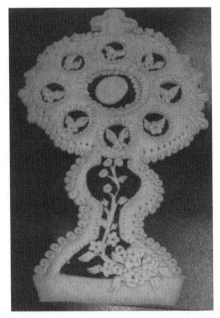

MONSTRANCE- Holds the Sacred Host
Sacred Heart Society Hall, Houston, Texas
Photo taken by Mary Anne Scanlan Grasso, March 2009

FAVA BEANS (dried)- "The Lucky Bean"
Sacred Heart Society Hall, Houston, Texas
Photo taken by Mary Anne Scanlan Grasso, March 2009

Photo of Mary Anne Scanlan Grasso, March 2012
Sacred Heart Society Hall, Houston, Texas

We Come to Your Feast

Verses

G   C

Cantor or choir:

1. We place up - on your ta - ble   a gleam-ing cloth of
2. We place up - on your ta - ble   a hum - ble loaf of
3. We place up - on your ta - ble   a sim - ple cup of
4. We ga - ther 'round your ta - ble,   we pause with - in our

G   C

white: the weav-ing of our   sto - ries,
bread: the gift of field and   hill - side,
wine: the fruit of hu - man   la - bor,
quest,   we stand be - side our   neigh - bors,

D

the fab - ric of our lives;   the dreams of those be -
the grain by which we're fed;   we come to taste the
the gift of sun and vine;   we come to taste the
we name the stran - ger "guest."   The feast is spread be -

G   Em   C

fore us,   the an - cient hope - ful   cries,
pres-ence   of him on whom we   feed,
pres-ence   of him we claim as   Lord,
fore us;   you bid us come and   dine:

G

the prom - ise of our fu - ture: our need - ing and our
to strength-en and con - nect us,   to chal-lenge and cor -
his dy - ing and his liv-ing,   his lead - ing and his
in bless - ing we'll un - cov-er,   in shar - ing we'll dis -

Am⁷   G

nur - ture   lie here be - fore our   eyes.
rect us,   to love in word and   deed.
giv - ing,   his love in cup out - poured.
cov - er   your sub - stance and your   sign.

Text: Michael Joncas, b.1951
Tune: Michael Joncas, b.1951
© 1994, GIA Publications, Inc.

AUTHENTIC ITALIAN RECIPES AND OTHER FAMILY FAVORITES

(*P SIGNIFIES PIZZITOLA FAMILY RECIPES, *S SIGNIFIES SACRED HEART SOCIETY RECIPES)

EAT & MANGIA!

APPETIZERS

CROSTINI

Louis Dimiceli

16 slices Italian bread (1/2 inch thick)
¼ cup virgin olive oil
1/3 cup black or green olives, pitted and chopped
½ lb. Mozzarella cheese (16 slices)
½ lb. plum tomatoes, cut lengthwise into 16 slices
1/8 teaspoon salt
1/8 teaspoon ground black pepper

Preheat oven to 400 degrees. Brush one side of bread slices with some of the olive oil. Bake until light brown and crusty, about 4 minutes. Spread the olives on each toast. Cover each slice with Mozzarella cheese and top with slice of tomato. Brush the tomato with remaining olive oil: sprinkle with salt and pepper. Bake until the cheese is melted, about 8-10 minutes. Serve at once. *P

ARTICHOKE APPETIZERS

Judy Pizzitola

2 (8 oz) cans Pillsbury crescent dinner rolls
¾ cup (3 oz.) shredded Mozzarella cheese
½ cup mayonnaise
1 (3 oz.) can (3/4 cup) grated Parmesan cheese
1 (14 oz.) can artichoke hearts, drained and finely chopped
1 (4 oz) can chopped green chilies, drained (optional)

Unroll dough into rectangles; press onto bottom and sides of 15x10x1 inch jellyroll pan to form crust. Bake at 375 degrees for 10 minutes. Combine remaining ingredients; mix well. Spread over crust. Bake at 375 degrees for 15 minutes or until cheese melts. Let stand for 5 minutes before serving. *P

FRIED MOZZARELLA

Mark Porter

1 lb. Mozzarella cheese (block)
Salt
Flour
Italian bread crumbs
2 eggs
Olive oil

Cut cheese into 3 x ½ inch strips. Dust with flour. Dip in egg to which salt has been added; coat with bread crumbs and fry in heated olive oil until golden brown on all sides. *P

CAPONATA

Louis Dimiceli

1/3 cup olive oil
3 medium onions, diced
5 large celery stalks, diced
2 large eggplants (about 4 lbs.), Peeled and diced
1/3 cup white wine vinegar
2 cups tomato puree
¾ cup pitted and quartered black olives Mediterranean)
½ cup rinsed capers, chopped
½ cup toasted pine nuts
½ teaspoon salt
Pepper to taste
Raisins, (optional)

Warm olive oil over medium heat in a very large sauce pan. Add the onion and celery; cook slowly, stirring occasionally, until very soft. Add eggplant and continue to cook until eggplant is completely wilted. Stir vinegar into saucepan. Add tomato puree; stir well and let simmer 10 minutes. Stir in olives, raisins, capers, pine nuts, salt and pepper; simmer an additional 5 minutes. Remove from heat and cool to room temperature or slightly cooled.

Can be made 2 or 3 days in advance and refrigerated. *P

ITALIAN STUFFED FRENCH BREAD

Terry Pizzitola

1 large loaf French bread
½ cup butter
¼ cup olive oil
10 cloves garlic, chopped
1 (10 oz.) pkg. frozen spinach, thawed and squeezed dry
½ cup coarsely chopped parsley
1 can artichoke hearts, drained and chopped
1 cup Mozarella cheese
2 Tablespoons capers, drained
¼ teaspoon tarragon
½ teaspoon basil
1 teaspoon black pepper

Cut top from French bread lengthwise and set aside. Scoop bread out of center of loaf and tear into small pieces. Heat butter and oil and add garlic. Add spinach, artichoke hearts, and parsley. Add to torn bread. Toss cheese, capers, and spices. Mix and put into hollow of bread. Put top on; wrap in foil. Bake at 350 degrees for 30 minutes. Unwrap; drizzle a little olive oil on top. Bake, uncovered, for an additional 5 minutes. Slice and enjoy. *P

PEPPERONI MONKEY BREAD

Judy Grasso Peplinski

1 package frozen Parker House rolls, cut in halves
2-3 oz. pepperoni (pizza style) chopped up
1 cup grated parmesan cheese
2 teaspoons dried oregano
½ teaspoon garlic powder
½ cup butter, melted
Mix above ingredients together, except butter, and set aside.

Spray bundt pan with cooking spray.
Cover half rolls with melted butter.
Coat rolls with dry mixture.
Layer with pepperoni in bundt pan.
Cover with dish towel and let rise until double in size—about 2-3 hours.

Bake in a 350 degrees oven for 25-30 minutes.

*This recipe can be used as a dessert with melted butter, and a cinnamon and sugar mixture. Both are great.

FAVORITE ARTICHOKE DIP

Judy Grasso Peplinski

2 (10 oz.) cans artichoke hearts in water (drained)
8 oz. grated parmesan cheese
2 teaspoons garlic powder
½ cup mayonnaise
2 Tablespoons dried parsley
1 pinch paprika

Place artichokes in a glass bowl. Mix in cheese, mayo, parsley, garlic powder and paprika.

Spray baking dish. Spread artichoke mixture evenly in baking dish. **Bake in 350 degrees oven** 25-35 minutes until bubbly. Serve hot.

BEST PATÉ

Stanley J. Peplinski

8 oz. cream cheese
1 ½ lbs. liverwurst
1 ½ lbs. fresh mushrooms, finely minced
2 Tbsp. butter
3 Tbsp. minced green onions
¼ tsp. garlic salt
1 tsp. seasoned salt
¼ tsp. black pepper
1 cup mayonnaise

Let cream cheese and liverwurst warm to room temperature.

Sauté mushrooms in butter until lightly browned.

While mushrooms are still warm, add all ingredients together.

Mix thoroughly.

Put in container with lid and refrigerate or freeze for later date.

SOUP & SALAD

AUNT ROSIE'S DELICIOUS TACO SOUP

Rosalie Grasso Macejewski

2 lbs. ground turkey or ground beef
½ package taco mix
1 medium onion, sliced
1 package Hidden Valley Ranch dressing mix
1 can pinto beans
1 can kidney beans
3 cans water
1 can stewed tomatoes
Grated cheddar cheese (optional)
1 can Ro-Tel (Original)

Brown meat and drain. Add all the other ingredients. Cook for 30 minutes. Serve hot with grated cheese, if desired, and tortilla chips. This recipe can be doubled, tripled, etc.

RUTH'S DELICIOUS V-8 SOUP

Ruth Lucas

Ingredients:

Large package stew meat, chopped in bite sizes
2 large cans V-8 juice, no water added
2 #2 cans whole tomatoes, chopped, with liquid
2 medium onions, cut in chunks
3 large potatoes to feed a bunch, cut in bite-size chunks
2 packages frozen soup vegetables (I like the one with okra, too)
Salt and pepper (only seasonings)

Instructions:

Cut fat off stew meat.

Salt and pepper meat and put in large pot.

Add V-8 juice, tomatoes and onions.

Bring to a boil. Simmer with lid until meat is tender.

Add potatoes.

Add salt and pepper to potatoes. Cover and simmer.

When potatoes are half way done, add frozen veggies. Cover and simmer until done.

Best when served with hot cornbread or French rolls.

THREE BEAN SALAD

Aunt Angeline Frenza Wall

1 (15 oz.) can cut green beans
1 (15 oz.) can yellow beans
1(15 oz.) can kidney beans
1 purple onion, sliced
1 green pepper, sliced
½ cup canola oil
½ cup apple cider vinegar
¼ cup sugar
1 teaspoon salt

Drain all beans and mix well in large bowl. Set aside.

Mix oil, vinegar, sugar and salt in pot.

Heat to blend.

When sugar is dissolved, pour over beans.

Mix well.

Refrigerate.

This is best if made the day before it is served.

Stir well.

JAZZED UP SALAD

Dianna Macejewski

1 (16 oz.) pre-packaged salad
8 bacon strips, cooked and crumbled
1 can (11 oz.) mandarin oranges, drained
½ cup vegetable oil
2 Tablespoons sugar
2 Tablespoons apple cider vinegar
¼ to ½ teaspoon salt

In a large salad bowl, toss the first six ingredients.

Combine the remaining ingredients in a jar with a tight-fitting lid; shake well.

Pour over salad and toss to coat.

AUNT ROSE ANN'S BROCCOLI SALAD

Rose Ann Scanlan Spudeck

1 large, fresh broccoli, washed and cut into bite-sized pieces
1 ½ oz. raisins
1 small red onion, cut in rings
1 cup Spanish peanuts
Mix and refrigerate

Do not add dressing until ready to serve

Dressing:

1 cup real mayonnaise

½ cup sugar

2 Tablespoons red wine vinegar

Blend and refrigerate

Just before serving, stir dressing into salad and serve

MARK'S MEXICAN CHICKEN SOUP

Mark Steven Grasso

Boil and de-bone a whole chicken. Add to chicken and broth:

cumin, chili powder, basil, oregano, salt, pepper, garlic, 6 whole allspice, parsley flakes, corn, potatoes, carrots, celery, stewed tomatoes, a can of Ro*Tel, canned green chilies, yellow squash, red, yellow and green bell peppers.

Stir well. Cook until vegetables are done. Serve with tortilla chips, grated Monterrey Jack cheese and lime. Garnish with cilantro and avocado.

VEGGIE

CANDIED YAMS

Yvonne Zeigman Grasso

Fresh (or large can(s), drained sweet potatoes
Brown sugar
Butter or oleo
Cinnamon

Bake fresh yams in 350 degrees oven about one hour or until done.

Peel and mash yams in buttered casserole dish.

Mix brown sugar, butter and cinnamon with yams.

Add a little extra brown sugar on top.

Heat thoroughly in 350 degrees oven.

Remove and top with marshmallows.

Return to oven and brown marshmallows.

Watch closely!

MARY ANN'S EGGPLANT PATTIES

Mary Ann Pizzitola Mustachio

1 medium-size eggplant
3 Tablespoons all-purpose flour
Salt and pepper
1 teaspoon baking powder
1 teaspoon grated onion
1 egg, beaten
½ cup cracker crumbs
Oil

Peel eggplant and cut into small pieces. Place eggplant pieces in a large saucepan and add to salted water to cover. Bring to a boil and cook until tender. Drain well and place eggplant in a large bowl. Mash eggplant and add onion, cracker crumbs, flour, baking powder and egg. Mix until just combined.

Heat 1 tablespoon of oil in a large skillet over medium-high heat. Drop eggplant batter by tablespoonfuls into hot skillet and fry until golden brown, turning once. Repeat to use all batter, adding more oil as needed. Serve warm. Makes 6 servings. *P

FRIED CARDUNI /CARDOON/ CARDONI (ARTICHOKE STALKS)

Madeline Frenza Grasso

2 artichoke stalks (looks like big celery)
1 big potato, peeled & cut in chunks

Coating:
2 eggs, beaten
1 teaspoon baking powder
1 cup flour
Milk, a little at a time
Salt & pepper to taste

Mix all ingredients together to get consistency of pancake batter. Can double or triple this recipe, if necessary.

Wash stalks well and remove leaves and strings—like cleaning celery. Cut into 6 inch strips about 1 inch wide. Keep in cold water until dropped in boiling water that has potato chunks. (This is to keep stalks from turning dark.) Boil until fork tender, but not falling apart. Drain in colander. Dip each piece in batter about the consistency of pancake batter. Fry in medium-hot oil. Drain on paper bag or paper towels. Serve immediately.

NONIE'S CANDIED YAMS

Beulah Nunn Scanlan
(Our family's favorite!)

Peel and cut up sweet potatoes. (I like to buy huge ones for the holidays
   and cut in big chunks.)
Keep them covered with water so they won't turn dark.
Spray pan or casserole with cooking spray and wipe out residue.
(I double this recipe for a large group.)
4 or 5 large sweet potatoes
1 cup white sugar
1 cup water
¼ stick Parkay
Approx. 2 teaspoons cinnamon

Pour sugar and water over raw potatoes.

Add cinnamon and dot with butter.

Bake uncovered @ 350 degrees for one hour, or until done and syrupy.

Turn yams over once after 30 minutes.

Enjoy!

MEMAW'S PINTO BEANS

Mary Anne Scanlan Grasso

2 pounds dried pinto beans
Ham bone with some ham or ham hocks or bacon
2 large yellow onions, cut in large chunks
2 large green bell peppers, cut in large chunks
Salt and pepper to taste
1 Tablespoon sugar

Sort dried beans and discard any small rocks or clods of dirt.

Wash beans thoroughly (I use a colander).

Place beans in large pot that has a lid.

Cover beans with water and lots to spare. (If necessary to add water later on, always boil water, first.)

Bring water to a boil. Turn fire down and simmer with lid.

When beans are getting soft, add salt, pepper and sugar.

About 30 minutes before beans are done, add onions and peppers.

These beans are great like this or as refried beans.

Refried Beans:

Put a small amount of oil in an electric skillet to keep beans warm before serving.

Add cooked beans with some juice.

Mash with potato masher.

Add grated cheese. (I prefer Longhorn Cheddar).

Salt and pepper, if necessary.

MAMA GRASSO'S FRIED FENNEL

(Fennochi Frittata)
Madeline Frenza Grasso

Wash and chop fresh fennel into small pieces, stems and fern

Boil fennel in salted water until tender.

Drain in colander

Fry one layer at a time in skillet with small amount of heated oil

Sprinkle small amount of flour and black pepper on each layer

Mix well

Hold skillet handle and shake often, so fennel won't stick

Brown one side, then place plate over fennel in skillet and flip over

Brown other side

Repeat until all fennel is cooked

Keep warm between two plates.

Serve hot.

(Variation—substitute flour with bread crumbs)

ITALIAN GREEN BEANS

Johanna Petronella
(Sacred Heart Member)

1 (28 oz.) can flat and wide Italian green beans; drain, don't rinse.
¼ cup dried bread crumbs
2 Tablespoons grated Parmesan or Romano cheese
Black pepper
Garlic, minced or garlic powder
2 Tablespoons olive oil

Spray casserole dish with cooking spray; wipe out with paper towel.

Mix together: green beans, bread crumbs, grated cheese, black pepper, garlic or garlic powder and olive oil. Put in prepared casserole dish.

Add more bread crumbs and olive oil on top (Optional)

Bake at 350 degrees until warm.

Variation: Spinach, squash, other vegetables could be substituted for the green beans. They can be fried as frittatas. Put enough olive oil to hold them together.

(Rosie Ragusa, another member, adds canned artichoke hearts, rinsed, to Johanna's green bean recipe.) *S

AUNT RUTH FRENZA'S STUFFED ARTICHOKES

Ruth Jensen Frenza

Trim tips off artichokes with kitchen scissors or sharp knife

Wash artichokes

Open leaves as wide as possible by hitting them against a cutting board

Steam artichokes, bottom down, in 2 or 3 inches of salted water on top of stove 10-15 minutes in pot with lid

In a large container, such as a roaster, mix together:

Dried, grated, bread crumbs (She uses a cheese grater)

Fresh garlic, finely chopped

Black pepper—lots—but no salt

Parmesan cheese, grated

In separate skillet, sauté diced onion in olive oil, set aside

Stuff artichokes with bread mixture

Spoon sautéed onion and olive oil over tops

Continue to steam artichokes on top of stove until done

MAMA GRASSO'S STUFFED ARTICHOKES

Madeline Frenza Grasso

(My precious mother-in law passed on good advice from her mother: "You can always add salt, but you can't take it away.")

Holding artichokes sideways, trim tips off artichokes with sharp knife.

Wash artichokes; Drain upside down.

Open leaves as wide as possible by hitting them against a flat surface.

In a big roaster pan, mix dried bread crumbs (French bread is best. If fresh baked, break in small chunks and dry in low oven. Then put in large plastic bag and crush with rolling pin until fine. (To make even finer crumbs, put through colander.)

Add fresh garlic, finely chopped.

Fresh onion, finely chopped.

Black pepper—lots—no salt, (most bread is salty enough).

Parmesan cheese (Don't overdo, like I did!)

Stuff artichokes with bread mixture.

Place artichokes, bottoms down, in roasting pan or large oven-proof container with lid.

Add enough water to half way up sides of artichokes. Do not cover tops. Cover with lid.

Bake in 350 degrees oven 1-1/2 hours until a leaf pulls out easily.

Spoon hot water from pan over tops of artichokes about 2 times while cooking.

Bread crumbs should be lightly browned when done.

(Mama Grasso never drizzled olive oil over tops while baking, but others have.)

MAMA GRASSO'S CRISPY CABBAGE

Madeline Frenza Grasso

Boil a large pot of salted water

Cut off stem of head of cabbage

Remove any wilted leaves.

Cut into four pieces or more if cabbage is large.

Wash cabbage pieces.

Boil cabbage until fork tender, but not falling apart.

Drain cabbage in colander.

Mix flour and salt and black pepper together.

Cover all sides of cabbage with flour mixture.

Fry in large skillet with ½ inch heated oil until

all sides are browned and crisp.

Drain on paper towels.

Enjoy!

MAMA GRASSO'S CRISPY CAULIFLOWER

Madeline Frenza Grasso

Boil a large pot of salted water.

Break apart a head of cauliflower into large pieces.

Wash pieces.

Boil cauliflower until fork tender, but still holding its shape.

Drain in colander.

Make an egg wash with one egg and small amount of water.

Mix flour, salt and pepper in separate dish.

Dip cauliflower in egg wash and then in flour.

Fry in heated olive oil until all sides are browned.

Yum!

MAMA GRASSO'S FRIED GREENS (FRITTATAS)

(Mustard, Collard, Turnip or etc.)
Madeline Frenza Grasso

Boil a large pot of salted water.

Clean, wash (in about three different sinks full of water) and cut up fresh greens.

Cook in boiling water with salt and pepper until tender.

Fry 3 or 4 slices of bacon chopped up with a small amount of chopped onion. Cook with greens.

Drain in colander.

Fry a layer at a time in a small amount of heated olive oil in skillet.

Sprinkle a small amount of flour, salt and black pepper over layer and mix.

Holding skillet handle, shake often to keep greens from sticking.

Brown one side.

Place a plate over layer of greens and flip it over to brown other side.

Keep greens warm between two plates.

(Some people substitute the flour with bread crumbs.)

STUFFED BAKED EGGPLANT

Madeline Frenza Grasso

1 fresh, medium-sized eggplant
Fresh garlic
Buffalo Mozzarella cheese
Olive oil

Peel eggplant.

Cut 2-inch-long slits about ½ inch deep alternately around the eggplant.

Soak eggplant in salted water for about 20-30 minutes to eliminate bitter taste.

Cut 2 or 3 pieces of garlic into slivers.

Cut cheese into inch-long slivers.

Rinse and dry eggplant.

Stuff cheese first, then garlic into slits.

Salt and pepper outside of eggplant.

Brown all sides of eggplant in ½ inch of olive oil in skillet.

Place in baking dish with lid with 1 or 2 inches of water.

Bake in 350 degrees oven about 45 minutes, turning once halfway through.

JUDY'S BAKED MUSHROOMS

Judy Grasso Peplinski

2 lbs. button mushrooms
1 stick real butter, softened—not melted
½ to 1 cup fresh parsley finely chopped
Garlic, minced—fresh or in a jar
Splash of soy sauce

Mix all ingredients in a bowl.

Wash mushrooms, cut off stems and turn mushrooms upside down in baking dish.

Stuff mixture in mushrooms.

Drizzle melted butter over tops of mushrooms.

Pour one cup of water in bottom of casserole dish.

Bake uncovered in 350 degrees oven for 20-30 minutes.

ZUCCHINI CASSEROLE

Charles Scanlan

Wash and slice 4 or 5 zucchini squash.

Slice ½ onion.

Steam both in pot on stove with very little water.

In separate pot, cook 1 can tomato sauce with mushrooms.

Add fresh sliced mushrooms.

Add ¼ teaspoon crushed dried oregano.

Add ¼ teaspoon dried basil.

Season to taste with salt and pepper.

Layer ½ zucchini and onion in prepared casserole dish.

Layer ½ tomato sauce on top.

Repeat layers.

Top with ½ -1 cup grated cheddar cheese.

Bake in 350 degrees oven about 20-30 minutes.

QUICK METHOD

Layer raw zucchini and raw onion in prepared casserole dish

Salt and pepper each layer

Pour ½ tomato sauce over top

Repeat

Top with grated cheese

Bake in 350 degrees oven about 30 minutes

EASY BAKED ASPARAGUS

Marie Scanlan Hamilton

1 lb. fresh asparagus
½ cup honey
½ cup real butter, melted
Salt and pepper

Trim and wash asparagus and place in a foil- lined casserole dish or pan. Salt and pepper to taste. Drizzle honey and melted butter over asparagus. **Bake in 350 degrees oven** for 15 minutes. Turn asparagus over and bake another fifteen minutes.

AUNT ANGELINA FRENZA'S CUCUZZA SQUASH

Submitted by Debbie Frenza

(Cacuzza squash is pale green in color and grows very long and very fast! My mother took some seeds to her brother-in-law. He was astounded at their rapid growth. He would measure them every day! The longest one I ever saw was about 30-36 inches long. Honest! They resemble a gourd, but are skinny around in comparison. They're very tasty.)

Peel and cut cucuzza in half or fourths, lengthwise, removing the seeds.

Cut in small pieces and set aside.

In large skillet, fry 4 strips bacon, cut up.

Add:

1 small onion, diced

1 (15 oz.) can stewed tomatoes

1 small can tomato paste

Season with salt and pepper and sugar

Cook 30 minutes on low heat, covered.

Add squash to mixture and cook, covered, about 15-25 minutes until squash is tender.

TRACY'S GRILLED ITALIAN VEGGIES

Tracy Lynn Peplinski

Olive oil
Fresh garlic, chopped
Onions, cut in big chunks
Yellow squash with peeling, sliced approx. ½ inch thick
Zucchini with peeling, sliced approx. ½ inch thick
Baby Portabello Mushrooms (whole)
Salt and pepper
Fresh Basil chopped finely (or substitute Basil paste)

Place all ingredients in a large bowl and toss together. Either grill outdoors kabob style or sauté in a skillet on the stove top.

FAVA BEANS

Internet

1 lb. dried fava beans
1 bunch green onions, chopped
1 medium onion, chopped
4 gloves garlic, chopped
3 bay leaves
Parsley, chopped
¼ cup olive oil
Salt and pepper to taste

Wash dried fava beans and cover with water. Cook in boiling water until tender, adding more boiling water as needed. Sauté seasonings in olive oil until tender then add to beans. Add salt and pepper to taste. Serve in soup bowls

MAIN DISH

CHICKEN PARMESAN

Judy Grasso Peplinski

4 boneless, skinless chicken breasts
½ cup olive oil
2 cloves garlic, chopped
¾ cup onion, chopped
1 large can crushed or diced tomatoes (28 oz. or larger)
1 teaspoon Italian seasoning
Olive oil
¼ teaspoon salt
¼ teaspoon pepper
1 Tablespoon sugar
½ cup Italian Style bread crumbs
2 eggs, beaten
½ cup shredded Mozzarella
¼ cup grated parmesan cheese

1. In a sauce pan, put 2 Tablespoons of olive oil.
   Add onion, garlic and sauté for a minute or two.
   Add tomatoes, Italian seasoning and sugar.
   Bring to a boil, and then simmer on low.

2. Between 2 sheets of wax paper, pound chicken to about 1/3 inch thick.

3. Beat eggs. Add salt and pepper.
   In separate bowl, mix bread crumbs, parmesan cheese and Italian seasoning.
   Dip chicken in egg mixture. Coat well.
   Roll chicken in bread crumb mixture.

4. Fry chicken in skillet with ½ cup hot olive oil over medium heat for 13 minutes.
    Drain on paper towels.

5. Place fried chicken on a cookie sheet. Place in 350 degrees oven for 13 minutes. Remove.
    Place a spoon full of tomato mixture on each piece of chicken.
    Top with shredded Mozzarella.
    Broil for 3-5 minutes until cheese is melted.
    Serve with pasta.

SLOW COOKER PORK ROAST

Elizabeth Peplinski Triplett

Pork roast
Salt and pepper
1 cup ground or finely chopped fresh cranberries
¼ cup honey
1 teaspoon grated orange zest
1/8 teaspoon ground cloves
1/8 teaspoon ground nutmeg
Sprinkle pork roast with salt and pepper.
Mix orange peel, cloves and nutmeg together.

Place roast in slow cooker.

Top with remaining ingredients.

Cook on low for 6 to 8 hours or until tender and delicious.

ITALIAN BEEF SANDWICHES

Cristy McCallum
(Cristy's grown son, Luke's, favorite!)

1 roast beef, approx. 2 ½ -3 pounds (I prefer rump or top round, may
    use chuck)
1 package dried Italian seasoning dressing mix
8 cloves garlic
1 small jar sliced banana peppers (6-8 oz.) and juice
1 cup water
Salt and pepper

Brown meat very well in skillet. Deglaze pan with water.

Place in slow cooker with juice.

Add remaining ingredients plus 1 teaspoon of salt and pepper.

Make sure you add juice from peppers.

Cook on high approx. 6-7 hours until meat falls apart.

Shred with fork and incorporate into juices.

Serve hot on good crusty buns with Mozzarella or Havarti cheese
on top.

Taste for additional seasoning.

This freezes very well.

QUICK & EASY HAMBURGER ITALIAN SANDWICHES

Mary Anne Scanlan Grasso

2 -3 pounds ground beef
1 medium onion, diced
Salt and pepper to taste
1 teaspoon dry Italian seasoning
Garlic powder to taste
French bread or Rolls
Mayonnaise

Brown meat with onions and seasonings. Drain.

Serve hot on good crusty rolls or French bread, sliced thick—spread with mayo.

Top with favorite grated cheese. (My favorite is Longhorn style Cheddar.)

SPICY CABBAGE STEW

Mary Anne Scanlan Grasso

2 lbs. ground beef
1 can Ro-Tel Green Peppers and Tomatoes (Original)
1 can Ranch Style beans with juice
½ green bell pepper, chopped
½ cup yellow onion, chopped
1 head cabbage, chopped
Salt and pepper
3-4 bean cans of water or beef broth (depends on size of cabbage)

In a large skillet, that has a lid, brown beef with onion, salt and pepper. Drain.

Add Ro-Tel, beans and water. Bring to a boil.

Add cabbage. Bring to a boil.

Simmer with lid about 15 minutes.

Serve hot with saltines or crusty bread.

ANGIE'S HERB CHICKEN

Angie Frank

3 large chicken breasts (I use boneless cut in half for 6 pieces)
1 can cream of chicken soup
¾ cup Sauterne wine (Sutters Home Chardonnay)
3 oz. mushroom pieces
¼ teaspoon thyme
¼ cup butter or oleo
1 (15 oz.) can water chestnuts, drained and sliced
2 Tbsp chopped green peppers
Salt and pepper to taste

Lightly season chicken with salt and pepper.

Brown chicken slowly in butter or oleo in skillet.

Arrange browned chicken in rectangular baking dish.

Add soup to drippings in skillet.

Slowly add wine to drippings, stirring till smooth.

Add remaining ingredients.

Heat to boiling.

Pour sauce over chicken.

Cover with foil and bake 350 degrees for 25 minutes.

Uncover and continue baking 25-30 minutes or until chicken is tender.

Long grain wild rice served with this is very good.

(This recipe can be doubled or tripled, etc.)

GOLDEN PORK CHOPS & POTATOES CASSEROLE

Sylvia Szabo

Hearty Meal-in- One that serves 8

Ingredients:

8 medium thick pork chops
4 large potatoes
2 cans Campbell's Golden Mushroom Soup
1 cup sharp shredded cheese
½ cup water
1 teaspoon Seasoned Salt

Instructions:

Wash/scrub potatoes; cut in medium-thick rings with skin. Set aside. In 9x13 baking pan arrange chops in single layer and brown, uncovered, **in hot oven (400-425 degrees)** for 2 minutes on each side. Remove chops from oven; add potatoes over the chops and shredded cheese over the potatoes. Sprinkle with Seasoned Salt. Spoon and spread the soup over all. Add the water at the corner of the pan. Cover with foil. **Bake in 375 degrees oven for 1 hour.**

Tips: Double the recipe for twice the number of servings; or, cut the recipe in half.

You may use an electric skillet instead of conventional oven. Cook at 300 degrees for 40 minutes.

PASTA MALANSA

Anna Marie Pizzitola Allen

Salt
2 Tbsp. pine nuts
1 fennel bulb (about 1 lb.), tops trimmed and bulb quartered
2 Tbsp. currants
4 cups tomato sauce (preferably homemade)
¾ cup extra virgin olive oil
Freshly ground pepper
1 lb. fresh sardines, filleted
¾ cups fresh bread crumbs
1 medium onion, chopped
1 lb. spaghetti
4 anchovy fillets, chopped

Fill a large pot with water; cover and bring to a boil. Add salt and the fennel and cook until tender, about eight minutes. Remove with a slotted spoon and finely chop, discarding the core. Reserve the water for cooking the pasta.

In a large saucepan, heat ½ of the olive oil. Add the sardines, onion, and anchovies and cook over moderately high heat, stirring, until the onion begins to brown, about five minutes. Add the fennel, pine nuts and currants and cook for three minutes. Add all but three tablespoons of the tomato sauce. Cover partially and cook over moderately low heat until thick, about 25 minutes. Season with salt and pepper; keep warm.

Meanwhile, heat the remaining1/4 cup of olive oil in a medium skillet. Add the reserved three tablespoons of tomato sauce and the bread crumbs and cook over moderately high heat, stirring until golden and crisp, about four minutes. Transfer to a plate. Return the pot of water to a boil. Add the pasta and cook until al dente; drain well. Return the pasta to the pot; add the sauce and toss over low heat for one minute. Transfer to a warmed platter. Top with ¼ of the bread crumbs and serve immediately. Pass the remaining crumbs at the table. *P

SIMPLE VERSION:

1 (15 oz.) can pasta con sarde (in yellow can at Antone's)
2 (3.75 oz.) cans sardines, filleted

Add the above to your homemade pasta sauce.

Brown plain Progresso bread crumbs in a cast iron skillet until golden brown. Add sugar and serve on top of pasta. *P

BOW TIE PASTA SURPRISE (FARFALLE)

Mary Anne Scanlan Grasso

1 (10 oz.) package Bow Tie pasta
2 lbs. Hot Jimmy Dean sausage
1 head cabbage, chopped
½ to 1 cup water
Ricotta or cottage cheese (Optional).

Boil pasta in salted water according to package directions. Drain.

Brown sausage in skillet and remove, leaving drippings.

Add water to sausage drippings.

Steam chopped cabbage in drippings.

Mix sausage with cabbage and pasta.

Serve hot,

Top with Ricotta or cottage cheese, if desired.

MELANESE SPAGHETTI SAUCE (MEATLESS)

Lillian Pizzitola
(Sacred Heart Society member)

Lillian says that the men members at the Hall make a huge amount of sauce for the feast day and she adds the following to **40 gallons of sauce.** This is her offering to St. Joseph. (It was absolutely delicious!)

3 (15 oz. cans) Pasta Con Sard concentrate made in Italy

3 huge cans sardines (twice as big as regular size—about 8 oz. per can) broken, <u>not</u> crushed

Boil fresh fennel—only the fern part. Save the water to boil pasta in later. Use about three cups of chopped, cooked fennel in the sauce.

Taste sauce. If not tasty enough, add 1 or 2 tubes (2 oz. size) of anchovy paste—or break up anchovies after the bones have been removed. (Gives special flavor of olive oil.)

Pasta Con Sard contents: Young fennel, water, sardines—(minimum 25%), raisins, onions, sunflower oil, salted sardines pureed. *S

MARIE'S BEST GOULASH

Marie King Matthews
(This is a great recipe to double for a large group, or
to give a casserole to a friend for any occasion.)

1 ½ -2 lbs. hamburger

1 large onion, diced

1 can cream of mushroom soup

1 can cream of chicken soup

1 can of whole kernel corn, drained

8 oz. sour cream

Pimientos, chopped—optional (or use Mexicorn with pimientos)

8 oz. bag of egg noodles

2 slices of buttered bread cut into croutons

Salt and pepper

Cook egg noodles in boiling water. Add a little oil to the water. Go easy on the salt as the soups are salty. Drain. In the meantime, brown the hamburger and onion. Add salt and pepper to taste. Drain grease and remove from heat. Add soups, corn, sour cream and pimientos. Layer in prepared oblong casserole, starting with small amount of meat then egg noodles. Top with 2 slices of buttered bread cut into croutons. **Bake in 350-375 degrees oven until bubbly hot and croutons browned.**

MARK'S PASTA

Mark Steven Grasso

In large skillet: Put about 4 Tablespoons olive oil.

Sauté eggplant (That has previously been peeled, cut into ¼ inch squares and set in salted water for several minutes, then rinsed.)

Add: 1 whole, red bell pepper, diced
1 purple onion, diced
Shallots, diced (optional)
Garlic, 2 or 3 cloves, chopped
Spinach, fresh, ½ bunch washed and chopped
Basil, lots, and if it's dry, crush it between fingers
Black pepper
Cracked red pepper (Pizza style)
Dash of vinegar

Boil pasta of your choice. Separate. Drain well.

Toss with sautéed mixture.

Add: parmesan cheese, black olives, feta cheese (optional), and ricotta (optional)

REAL SICILIAN PIZZA –FACCIA DI VECCHIA—OLD LADY'S FACE

Aunt Annie Grasso Ciulla Listi

Make a yeast dough for pizza, or substitute Hot Roll Mix. One box makes a 9x13 Pyrex dish, (2 layers) or use two boxes for a cookie sheet with sides. **Go by <u>pizza</u> directions on the box.**

Let dough rise once in bowl before you put it in pan. One large bowl per box.

Assemble and prepare all ingredients before making dough. Kneading time is only five minutes and another five minutes to sit before adding ingredients.

Ingredients:

2 Large cans diced tomatoes
Hamburger and ground, lean pork loin—use half amount of each
Green onion, chopped
Fresh garlic, crushed
Salt and pepper
Romano cheese cut in small cubes and some grated
Anchovies cut in small pieces
Oregano
Olive oil
Grated dry bread crumbs (We used plain croutons crushed up. Works great!)

Directions:

1. Drain can tomatoes, dice, cook in skillet until thickens. Set aside to cool.
   Next, cook meat loose in skillet with a little bit of chopped green onion, crushed garlic, salt and pepper
2. Drain and cool meat. Cover so won't dry out and set aside.
3. Grease pan or dish with shortening.
4. Fill up pan with ½ of dough.

First Layer:

Anchovies (not for the faint-hearted!) small pieces pinched into dough with cubes of Romano cheese.

Half of stewed tomatoes, meat mixture, grated Romano cheese.

Second Layer:

Repeat process. Then sprinkle a little black pepper—NO SALT--!

Top with grated, dry bread crumbs, oregano, pepper, olive oil.

Cover with dish towel and let rise in pan.

Heat oven at 350 degrees. Bake until done. Takes about 45-60 minutes to cook dough thoroughly.

MARY ANNE'S LASAGNA

Mary Anne Scanlan Grasso

2 large **onions** diced, one for sauce, one for meat
5 or 6 cloves of **garlic**, diced, half for sauce, half for meat
2 pounds **hamburger meat**
Salt and pepper to taste

Brown hamburger with one onion, 2 or 3 cloves of chopped garlic, salt and pepper.

Add:

1 teaspoon oregano leaves
1 teaspoon celery seed
1 teaspoon anise seed
1 or 2 large bay leaves

When meat is done, remove grease and set aside.

In skillet, sauté the remaining chopped onion and garlic in **2 Tablespoons olive oil.**

Add:

2 regular size cans or 1 large can of tomatoes, diced. (I use a potato masher to chop them up fine after dicing them.)

2 large cans tomato paste, cook for a couple minutes

4 tomato paste cans of water

Transfer sauce and meat to large pot.

Add:

Salt, pepper, sugar* to taste, Add 1 teaspoon each of oregano leaves, celery seed, anise seed and two more bay leaves to sauce. Bring to a boil, stirring constantly. Then, simmer with lid for a couple of hours or more. Stir occasionally.

Grate 16 ounces **Mozzarella cheese** and 16 ounces **Cheddar cheese (I prefer Longhorn style Cheddar** because my mother always used it and I love the taste.)

Boil **1 box of Lasagna** with a few drops of oil to keep it separate. Stir. Follow package directions. Al Dente.

Drain pasta in colander. While still hot, place single layers between **foil paper**. (This keeps pasta warm and it doesn't stick together.)

(I use Pam spray on bottom and sides of a 9 x 13 casserole dish and wipe it out with a paper towel.)

Starting with a thin layer of sauce, layer lasagna, **grated Romano/ Parmesan cheese,** meat sauce, and two cheeses. Repeat in same order.

Bake in preheated oven at 375 degrees until bubbly hot through and through and cheeses melted.

*My husband is Sicilian and prefers sweet sauce. So I add about ½ cup of sugar for one recipe. I always double this recipe to feed 16-18 people. Of course, we have salad, garlic bread and desserts, too! **Enjoy!**

LEMONY ORZO

Yvonne Zeigman Grasso

8 ounces orzo pasta, uncooked
3 tablespoons olive oil
1 clove garlic, sliced
1 ½ teaspoons lemon zest
2 tablespoons lemon juice
3 tablespoons minced parsley
¼ cup grated Parmesan cheese
¼ cup slivered, pitted kalamata olives
¼ cup sliced scallions
Freshly ground black pepper, to taste

Instructions:

Boil orzo pasta until al dente; drain.

In a non-stick skillet, heat olive oil and garlic, over low heat until garlic is lightly golden, about 2 minutes. Raise heat to medium and stir in orzo, lemon zest, lemon juice, and parsley. Cook, stirring, until pasta is hot.

Remove from heat; stir in Parmesan cheese, kalamata olives, and scallions. Add freshly ground black pepper to taste. Makes 4 servings.

MOZZARELLA CASSEROLE

Betty Ann Scanlan

Cook and drain 1 package wide egg noodles

Cook 3 lbs. ground beef or ground turkey with ½ diced onion and diced garlic till done.

Season to taste

Drain.

Add 3 (14 oz). bottles of pizza sauce to meat and stir in 1 lb. grated Mozzarella cheese.

Mix well.

Put in casserole dish and top with grated Mozzarella cheese.

Bake @ 350 * for 20-30 minutes

VEAL SCALLOPINI

Elizabeth Cuccerre

2 lbs. veal cutlets, pounded to about ¼ inch and cut into medallions
1 cup Marsala or sherry wine
½ cup flour
1 cup chicken or beef broth
1 teaspoon salt
½ lemon
¼ teaspoon black pepper
1 teaspoon oregano

Sprinkle the veal with salt and pepper and place in glass bowl. Pour over medallions the Marsala or sherry wine. Marinate, covered, in refrigerator for 1 hour (1 ½ hours at most). Drain the medallions, reserving the wine. Dip medallions in flour and brown them in a stick of butter in large skillet. When browned, add chicken or beef broth, juice of ½ lemon, the reserved wine, and oregano. Simmer for 8 to 10 minutes. (Stir the sauce every so often while cooking).*S

CURRIED SHRIMP

Sue Wyche

Mix in skillet:
¼ cup real butter
¼ cup flour
½ teaspoon salt
1/16 teaspoon paprika
1 teaspoon curry powder
Dash of cayenne pepper
Add: 1 ½ cups milk
3 Tablespoons catsup
¼ cup sherry

Stir until thickened. Add one pound cooked, cleaned shrimp. Stir until hot. Serve over a bed of cooked rice.

BEST FRIED SHRIMP

Helen Dyer Scanlan

Clean and wash shrimp, drain

Make crumbs out of fresh saltine crackers

Beat raw eggs in separate bowl

Dip shrimp in egg, then in cracker crumbs

Fry in hot oil

Drain on paper towels

Salt to taste

"You'd better make a lot!"

BAKED REDFISH

Mary Charlet
(St. Joseph Altar recipe)

3 ripe tomatoes
Dash of sugar
3 garlic cloves
1 tsp. oregano
1 small onion
½ tsp rosemary leaves
1 carrot
2 Tbsp. Parmesan cheese
1 stalk celery
1 (8 oz.) can tomato sauce
1 tsp. parsley
8 oz. water
Salt and pepper
1 (3 to 5 lb.) redfish

Chop tomatoes and put into pan with vegetables that are finely chopped. Add parsley, salt and pepper, and sugar. Add tomato sauce and 8 oz. water. Simmer until the ingredients have cooked to a nice consistency. Pour sauce over fish to be baked. Add lemon slices. Bake at 350 degrees for 1 ½ hours or until tender.

TEX MEX

MEMAW'S TACOS

Mary Anne Scanlan Grasso
(You can always add more seasoning—you can't take it away!)

2-3 pounds ground beef
1 large yellow onion, diced
Salt and pepper to taste
Garlic powder to taste
Ground cumin to taste—I use a lot! (Start with 2 teaspoons.)
White corn tortillas
Lettuce & tomatoes
Grated cheddar or sliced American cheese strips (I prefer Longhorn cheddar)
Picante sauce

Salad:

Slice lettuce and dice tomatoes and refrigerate. Wait to salt and pepper until serving.

Brown meat with onion and seasonings. Salt and pepper to taste. Drain and set aside.

Place tortilla in small amount of heated oil in skillet. After a couple of seconds, flip over and put some taco meat in center of tortilla and fold in half. I use a large skillet and make three tacos at a time. Brown folded taco on one side and flip over to brown other side. (Watch out for onions; they pop!) Drain on paper towels. Serve hot.

Let each person fill tacos with salad, cheese and picante.

I like to add 5 or 6 raisins to each of my own tacos. I love them this way!

EASY CHEESE ENCHILADAS

Mary Anne Scanlan Grasso
Feeds 2 or 3 people

1 dozen white corn tortillas
1 can Hatch Tex-Mex Enchilada Sauce—Medium
½-1 small yellow onion, diced
8 oz. Longhorn Cheddar cheese, grated

Grate cheese and dice onion. Set aside.

Spray pan or oven dish with cooking spray and wipe out residue.

Warm sauce in pot on the stove.

Dip each tortilla in sauce, one at a time and lay it flat on pan.

Top with small amount of onion and cheese and a Tablespoon of sauce.

Repeat above stacking like pan cakes.

Pour any remaining sauce over enchiladas.

Make 2 six-layer stacks, or 3 four-layer stacks or whatever.

Bake in 350 degrees oven for 15-20 minutes. Serve hot.

Garnish around the edge of the plate with fresh Romaine lettuce.

1 or 2 fried eggs on top is a real treat. (Optional)

NONIE'S ONE–OF-A-KIND TACOS

Beulah Nunn Scanlan
(A sweet lady from Mexico taught my Mama how to
make these in the 40's. My brothers would see who
could eat the most! Everyone loved them.)

Taco Mixture

1 lb. ground beef
1 small onion, diced
1 small can tomato sauce
1 teaspoon ground cumin
2 Tablespoons apple cider vinegar
½ teaspoon salt
¼ teaspoon black pepper
Pinch of sugar
1 dozen corn tortillas

Raisins (optional) I add 5 or 6 raisins inside my taco, sometimes. My Mama cooked one pan with raisins and one skillet without raisins. Both are delicious.

Salad—make ahead and refrigerate

Mix together:

2 cups shredded cabbage
2 Tablespoons Miracle Whip
1 tomato, diced
Salt and pepper to taste

Put ground meat in a skillet with no grease. Add onion, salt, pepper, sugar and cumin. Fry until cooked. Drain grease. Add vinegar and tomato sauce. Continue to cook for a few minutes. Remove from heat. In another skillet, add about 2 Tablespoons of oil. Get it hot, then add one flat tortilla in the oil for a couple seconds. Then, turn it over and add meat mixture. Fold over and fry on both sides until browned. Drain on paper towels. When ready to serve, add salad and enjoy!

SWEET AUNT PATTI'S SPANISH RICE

Patricia Scanlan Ortega

2 cups raw rice
4 ½ cups boiled chicken broth (use broth and chicken from 5 or 6 boiled
    chicken wings. Shred chicken and discard skin after cooking.)
1 can tomato sauce
3 Tablespoons onion, chopped
1 teaspoon salt
¼ teaspoon black pepper
1 teaspoon ground cumin
½ teaspoon garlic salt or garlic powder
2 Tablespoons oil

Brown rice slowly in hot oil. Stir constantly until browned. Just before
rice is browned, add onion and cook.

Once the rice is browned, <u>do not</u> stir again.

Add tomato sauce, boiling hot broth and shredded chicken. **Do not stir!**

Add seasonings on top. **Do not stir!**

Cover and simmer for 35 minutes.

Remove from heat.

Stir when ready to serve.

SPECIALTY

NONIE'S MOIST CORNBREAD DRESSING

Beulah Nunn Scanlan
(Our family's favorite)

Make a double batch of cornbread a day or two before you need it.

(I use Aunt Jemima's yellow cornbread recipe on bag only I add ¼ cup sugar.)

Boil turkey or chicken giblets or turkey/chicken wings (with skin) with salt and pepper in pot of water.

Save broth. Can add canned chicken broth, if necessary.

Crumble up cornbread in a very large pan or casserole you will bake it in.

Add:

Chopped giblets and/or skinless wings, chopped
1 large yellow onion, diced
1 large green bell pepper, diced
2 cups celery, chopped

Add:

1 teaspoon salt
½ teaspoon black pepper
1 teaspoon ground poultry seasoning (A little goes a long way!)

Add broth from boiled giblets and extra broth, if necessary, to <u>make really mushy</u> and you'll never have dry dressing again!

Mix well.

Bake in 350 degrees oven for about 40 minutes, until lightly brown on top.

UNCLE PETE FRENZA'S RICOTTA

Charon Frenza Wimp

½ gallon milk
1 pint buttermilk
2 cups water
Salt to taste
1 Tablespoon sugar

Cook until curdles form. Drain liquid.

BEBE'S BEST BLUEBERRY PANCAKES

Judy Grasso Peplinski

(Six-year-old J. T. says, "I can make these!")

Martha White's Blueberry Muffin Mix

Follow recipe on package for muffins—(egg and milk), but add 1 ½ Tablespoon flour.

Mix only until moist—leave lumps!

Spray skillet or griddle.

Drop by spoonfuls onto griddle.

Brown each side.

Enjoy with butter and syrup or whatever you like. **Yum!**

This recipe can be doubled, etc.

FRIED BREADCRUMBS—MOLLICA/ MUDICA/MUDRICA—(SAWDUST)

Madeline Frenza Grasso

Dry a good quality bread for breadcrumbs. (I prefer French bread that has some salt in it.)

Fresh bread can be broken into pieces and put on cookie sheets in a 250 degrees oven to dry.

Dried bread can be put in a plastic bag or between wax paper and crushed with rolling pin or put into a blender or food processor. Then, for finer crumbs place in colander.

Put some olive oil in large skillet, just enough to coat pan. Add breadcrumbs, stirring constantly over medium heat. Add black pepper and sugar to taste. If bread is salty enough, no need to add more. Remove from skillet immediately when browned. Put in bowl to cool. Store in refrigerator in large Ziploc type bag. Will keep for months.

Serve over pasta with sauce. (We prefer the sweet taste of sauce and the sweet taste of breadcrumbs, so I add more sugar to mine.)

ST. JOSEPH'S BREAD—PANE DI SAN GIUSEPPE (PANNE GROSSE)

Internet
Copyright 1995-2012 **The Kitchen Link, Inc.**
All Rights Reserved-**www.recipelink.com-**

St. Joseph's Bread is a traditional bread served on St. Joseph's Day, March 19. It is an egg bread with a crumb that has a tighter, denser weave, allowing the dough to be used for fancy bread-sculpting designs. Breads in the forms of crosses, staffs, wheat sheaves, images of St. Joseph, and braids of the Blessed Mother adorn the St. Joseph's table and are eaten throughout the feast day. (**Do not confuse this recipe with the one below that is inedible.**)

Yield: 2 loaves, about 1 1/3 pounds each
Preparation Time: 30 minutes
Rising Time: first, about 2 hours; second, about 1 hour
Baking Time: 30 minutes

Proofing Mixture:

½ **cup warm water**
1 Tablespoon active dry yeast
1 teaspoon sugar or honey

For the Dough:

7 cups unbleached all-purpose flour
1 tablespoon salt
2 cups water
3 tablespoons extra-virgin olive oil, divided
4 large eggs, beaten slightly

For the Work Surface and Baking Sheets:

Extra flour for work surface and kneading (if necessary)
½ cup yellow or white cornmeal

For the Egg Wash:

1 whole egg
1 tablespoon water

1. To proof the yeast, pour ½ cup warm water into a small bowl. Sprinkle the yeast and sugar over the surface, and stir with a fork for about 30 seconds. Let stand for 5 minutes, until the mixture is frothy. (If the yeast does not froth, it is no longer active and should be discarded.)
2. While the yeast is proofing, place the flour and salt in a large bowl and stir to combine. Make a deep hole in the center of the flour by pushing flour up the sides of the bowl. Pour the proofed yeast mixture, the 2 cups water, 2 tablespoons of the olive oil, and eggs into the well in the flour.
3. Holding the edge of the large bowl with one hand, use the other hand to mix the liquid into the flour. Starting from the center, slowly work your way around the bowl, incorporating a little of the flour at a time. Keep going around until all the flour and liquid is combined to form a soft dough. Rub the extra dough clinging to your hand into the mixture. If the dough is too sticky, add a little more flour, a tablespoon at a time, until the stickiness is gone. If there is flour left in the bowl, add a little more water,
    1 tablespoon at a time, until all the ingredients are combined into a non-sticky mound of dough.
4. Turn the dough out onto a lightly floured surface. Lightly oil your hands to prevent the dough from sticking. This dough needs to be firmer than the other bread dough; knead more

flour into it. The firmer the dough, the easier it is to get more definition in your sculpted bread. It will not rise as much, allowing you to make more intricate designs.

5. To knead, divide the dough in half. Knead for about 10 to 15 minutes. The dough will become smooth, elastic, and satiny.

6. Place 1 tablespoon olive oil in the palm of your hand and rub the oil over the entire surface of the dough. Place the dough in a large, unscented plastic bag. Push all the air out of the bag and close it at the top with a twist tie, leaving room for the dough to rise and double in bulk inside the bag. Place in a draft-free warm spot ((about 80 degrees F) to rise.

7. In about 1 ½ hours, the dough should be ready. To check on its progress press two fingertips about ½ inch into the dough. If the indentations remain when your fingertips are removed, the dough is ready. Punch the dough down and knead briefly to distribute the air bubbles, about 30 seconds.

8. Sprinkle 2 tablespoons cornmeal on each of two 17x11-inch baking sheets. Divide the dough into two portions and form loaves. Place the loaves on the baking sheets. Brush top with egg wash. Allow enough room for each to double in size. The second rising will take about 1 hour.

9. Prepare the oven by arranging an oven rack on the bottom shelf and the other on the second from the top shelf. Preheat the oven to 400 degrees F.

10. Place one baking sheet on the bottom rack and bake for 15 minutes, then transfer it to the upper rack, baking for an additional 15 minutes. Place another baking sheet on the bottom rack. This is my staggering technique of baking, making the best use of the oven space, allowing you to be more efficient. The loaves will take 30 minutes to bake. You will know the bread is done if it makes a hollow sound when you tap on it or by its golden brown color.

11. When done, remove the bread from the baking sheets immediately and place on wire racks or kitchen towels to cool.

NOTES: If you are going to use the bread on the same or following day, store the loaves at room temperature in a brown paper bag. This will help retain a good crust. The bread will keep fresh this way for up to 2 days.

-This bread freezes very well and will keep in the freezer for up to 3 months. Wrap individual loaves in heavy-duty aluminum foil and place in reclosable plastic freezer bags. To reheat frozen bread, remove plastic bag and allow to defrost at room temperature. Place unwrapped bread directly on the oven rack in a preheated 350 degrees oven for 7 to 10 minutes.

INEDIBLE DOUGH RECIPE—FOR SCULPTING ALTAR SYMBOLS

Internet-Italiansrus.com

This bread –type dough is often used to sculpt the intricate religious symbols for the Saint Joseph Table/Altar. (See Glossary for different types of symbols.) They can be stored in pizza boxes and frozen to be used year after year.

5 lbs. flour
1 lb shortening
Water, only enough to form firm dough

Combine all ingredients. Knead and roll out as thin as possible yet large enough to cut out the desired shape. You need two of these shapes. Once your shape is ready, add the fig filling to the dough and place the second piece of dough directly over the fig filling. Use your creative ability and begin to create a design by cutting out the top layer of the dough. Once you are done being creative you will bake it in a low heat oven until it turns to light brown.

FIG FILLING FOR INEDIBLE DOUGH

Purchase one circle of dried figs

Soak figs in warm water for about 10-15 minutes

Remove stem from each fig

Grind figs

If you like, you may add raisins

Do not refrigerate paste if you plan to use it soon. It becomes too stiff to work.

DESSERTS

AUNT PILL'S SESAME SEED COOKIES (GIUGGUILANI)

Phyllis Frenza Marino

4 ½ cups flour
4 teaspoons baking powder
½ teaspoon salt
2 cups sugar
½ cup shortening
3 teaspoons vanilla
4 eggs slightly beaten
2 or 3 jars (about 2 oz. size) sesame seeds

Toast sesame seeds in dry skillet until golden brown, stirring constantly. Place on paper towels. (Seeds will _not_ brown more while baking. Don't expect to use leftover toasted seeds later on—they turn rancid!)

Directions:

Sift dry ingredients. Set aside. Cream shortening and sugar in mixer. Add eggs and vanilla. Add dry ingredients to creamed mixture.

Roll out as much dough as you can handle in a rope fashion. (As thin as a pencil)

Cut 2 inches long. Roll in toasted sesame seeds, covering outside thoroughly.

Place on cookie sheets covered with parchment paper.

Bake 375 degrees oven about 10 minutes.

Can bake two trays at a time, switching trays after five minutes.

EASY KEY LIME PIE

Rosalie Grasso Macejewski

1 largest size graham cracker crust or 2 small ones
2 Key Lime Yoplait yogurts
1 small box Sugar-free Lime Jell-O
¼ cup boiling water
1 (12 oz.) carton Cool Whip

Unwrap all packaging. Boil water and add to Jell-O in large bowl. Use whisk to dissolve.

If necessary, place bowl in microwave for a few seconds to dissolve Jell-O completely. Stir in yogurt. Mix well. Stir in Cool Whip. Mix well.

Pour into pie crust.

Chill.

Substitute any flavor yogurt and matching Jell-O.

AUNT ANNIE'S PIGNOLLATTI

(Pine cones)
Angeline Grasso Ciulla Listi
(submitted by Angel Grasso Strubing)

3 cups flour
½ teaspoon salt
2 level teaspoons baking powder
Sift dry ingredients together and set aside.
4 eggs, beaten
2 Tablespoons cream

Mix well.

Add dry ingredients to creamed mixture. Mix well.

Cut dough in pieces and roll in 12 inch lengths. (pencil size)

Let dry for awhile and cut into small pieces, about one inch

Fry in hot oil. Place fried pieces on greased pan.

In iron skillet, melt **two cups sugar**.

Pour sugar over pieces and shape like pine cones. (They harden when cool.)

*Angel adds a few drops of honey to cooked sugar to keep it from getting hard.

Angel says they shaped them in small clusters.

Aunt Phyllis Marino shaped them into stacks (pine cones).

MY MAMA'S SFINGE/ SPHINGE DOUGHNUTS

Madeline Frenza Grasso
(Submitted by Rosalie Grasso Macejewski)

3 eggs
1 cup sugar
1 cup milk boiled and cooled
1 teaspoon vanilla
3 cups flour, sifted with next two items
2 teaspoons baking powder
1 teaspoon salt

Beat eggs until light. Gradually add sugar. Add cooled milk.

Add vanilla, then dry ingredients.

Drop by spoonfuls in hot shortening or oil. Fry until brown.

Remove and drain on paper towels.

Sprinkle with powdered or granulated sugar. Serve warm.

NEVER FAIL PIE CRUST

Mary Anne Scanlan Grasso
(This makes three single pie crusts. Can be bagged and refrigerated.)

Sift together:

3 cups flour
1 teaspoon salt

Add:

1 ¼ cups Crisco shortening

Mix these ingredients with a pastry blender until crumbly. Set aside.

In cup, beat with fork:

5 Tablespoons ice water
1 teaspoon apple cider vinegar
1 egg

Add to flour mixture with pastry blender.

Roll out on lightly-floured surface. (Handle gently. The more you handle pie dough, the tougher it is!) Place pie crust in pie plate for single or double- crust pies. **Fill pie plate and bake in 400 degrees oven.** Watch it closely!

MOTHER ROSE'S LEMON PIE

Rose Melody Scanlan
(My precious paternal grandmother's Blue Ribbon
winner at a Wisconsin State Fair!)

Bake your pie crusts first and set aside. (See Never Fail Pie Crust recipe).

Put two cups of water into a pan and bring to a boil. Dissolve ½ cup corn starch in 1 cup of cold water and add to boiling water, stirring constantly until thickens and is clear. Set aside

For two pies:

6 eggs
2 lemons
1 cup sugar
½ teaspoon salt

Separate 4 eggs. Put 4 yolks and 2 whole eggs in mixer and beat well. Put in pot. Save 4 egg whites in refrigerator for meringue (See No-Weep Meringue recipe).

Grate the yellow rind from lemon. (Not the white part!). Remove juice from lemons. Add the grated rind and juice to the eggs. Add sugar and salt. Place pot over slow fire. Cook slightly, stirring constantly so it won't stick. Add corn starch mixture to eggs.

Cook, stirring until well blended and thickened. Pour into cooked pie crusts.

Top with meringue. Bake 375-400 degrees oven until meringue nicely browned.

BEST PECAN PIE

Madeline Frenza Grasso

1 cup white Karo syrup
½ cup sugar
2 eggs
2 Tablespoons flour
2 tablespoons Parkay
½ teaspoon real vanilla
2 cups pecans, chopped

Preheat oven at 375 degrees.

Partially bake pie crust—about 5 minutes.

Put eggs in pot and beat a little.

Add: sugar, vanilla, syrup and oleo, stirring while adding. Mix in flour, a little at a time, stirring constantly to keep from lumping. Do not cook—just melt oleo. Remove from heat.

Add chopped pecans.

Pour into partially-baked pie crust.

Bake until crust is browned, about 20-22 minutes. Don't over bake.

CHERRY CAKE BROWNIES

Bessie Spedale

1 (2-layer size) pkg. fudge cake mix
1 (21 oz. can cherry pie filling
1 teaspoon almond extract
2 eggs, beaten
1 pkg. chocolate chips
5 Tablespoons butter
1 cup sugar
1/3 cup milk

Preheat oven to 350 degrees.

In a large bowl, mix cake mix, almond extract, pie filling and eggs. Beat well. Pour into greased, floured 13x9x2 inch baking dish. Bake 20 to 30 minutes. Remove. Cool 1 to 2 hours before frosting.

Frosting: Bring sugar, butter and milk to boil for 1 minute. Remove from heat; add chocolate chips. Stir until chips melt. Spread over cooled brownies.*S

WEDDING RING COOKIES

Damiana Zuchero
(Sacred Heart Society Ladies' President)

8 cups flour, sifted
1 ½ cups granulated sugar
1 ½ cups shortening
1 teaspoon baking powder
½ cup buttermilk (start with ½ cup and add more if necessary to get
    proper consistency)

Mix all ingredients by hand. (No mixer.) Roll a small amount of dough
on a surface until thickness of a pencil. Wrap around pointer finger and
pinch off excess dough. Place on ungreased cookie sheet. **Bake in 325
degrees oven until done**. (This recipe makes **a lot** of cookies.)

WEDDING RING COOKIE ICING

Icing is just powdered sugar, food coloring and Anise flavoring **if** you like Anise. It's a strong flavor and one drop is all you need.

Cook on low heat, stirring constantly until crystallized.

Dip cookies in hot sugar and place on wax paper until icing is hard.

(Sometimes I add milk to my powdered sugar and it gives it a thicker icing.)

Dough refrigerates well for a couple days. Keep baked cookies in airtight containers.

ITALIAN FIG COOKIES (CUCCIDATI)

Father Charles Samperi
St. James the Apostle Catholic Church—Spring Texas

Cookie Dough

8 cups sifted flour
1 ½ cups shortening
1 cup sugar
3 eggs
3 Tablespoons baking powder
1 cup milk, approximately
¼ teaspoon salt
1 ½ teaspoons vanilla extract
1 ½ teaspoon Anise flavoring

Sift flour, measure, and resift with sugar, baking powder, and salt. Cut in shortening with fingers until mixture resembles cornmeal. Make a well in the flour and break eggs into it. Add half of milk and both flavorings. Knead well for 5 minutes, adding the rest of the milk gradually as you knead. Add only enough milk to make a medium soft dough, which is easy to handle. Divide dough into 3 parts. Roll out dough until it is about ¼ inch thick. Cut into strips about 3 inches wide. Roll out fig mixture into a rope, a little smaller than one inch. Place fig mixture in center of the dough. Fold dough over, making sure the edges are sealed. Cut into cookies about 2 inches long. Place on cookie sheet and bake at 375 degrees for about 18 to 25 minutes. Remove from oven and frost while hot. Makes 10 dozen cookies.

NOTE: this dough is excellent for anise rolls. Shape into the size of a finger. Place on a cookie sheet 1 inch apart. **Bake in moderate oven 375 degrees until lightly brown, about 8 to 10 minutes.**

Filling

4 pkgs. dried figs (remove stems from figs and grind figs and raisins)
½ box of raisins
1 orange with juice and peel (zest)
1 ¼ teaspoon ground cloves
2 teaspoons cinnamon
¼ to ½ cup port wine
2 cups honey
1 cup walnuts, pecans and almonds, finely chopped

Frosting

4 egg whites beat until stiff
Add ¼ teaspoon cream of tartar, anise or vanilla
3 or 4 cups of confectionary sugar (tint with white, red, green food coloring)

Frost cookies with sprinkles

ITALIAN FIG COOKIES (CUCCIDATE)

Aunt Ruth Jensen Frenza

Dough:

8 cups flour, sifted
1 teaspoon salt
1 ½ cups Crisco
1 ½ cups sugar
1 ½ cups wine (we use Manischewitz blackberry or grape)

Filling:

2 oranges, zest and juice
4 lbs. dried figs
1 lb. dates
1 lb. raisins
1 ½ cups sugar dissolved in 1 ½ cups wine
3 teaspoons cinnamon
1 teaspoon black pepper

Remove stems from figs, first. Grind up figs, dates, and raisins. Add a little wine to dried fruit as you grind to soften them. (Add a little more wine to dough and/or filling if necessary)

Assembly Directions:

Roll out a portion of dough as thin as possible on a lightly floured surface. Cut a 3-4 inch wide strip. With your fingers, place filling in center of strip. Fold over both sides towards center. Flip over and flatten entire strip slightly with rolling pin. Cut cookies as desired to resemble Fig Newtons. (Aunt Ruth cuts slits on one side of cookie, and then twists each part to resemble a lovely flower.)

Grease pans or use parchment paper. **Bake 350 degrees oven for about 20 minutes.** (Can bake two trays at one time, switching trays after 10 minutes.) Store in tightly closed glass jars for best results. Left over filling can be refrigerated for months.

KRINGLE—LOW SUGAR COFFEE CAKE

Linda A. Smith

Layer I

½ cup margarine
1 Tablespoon sugar
1 Tablespoon flour
2 Tablespoons water
Mix above ingredients like pie dough.
Spread on a cookie sheet in 2 strips, 3 inches wide.

Layer II

Boil:

1 cup water
½ cup margarine
Stir in 1 cup flour

Add 3 eggs, one at a time, beating well after each. Add 1 Tablespoon sugar and ½ teaspoon almond extract. Spread over Layer I. (It's like cream puffs). **Bake at 375 degrees for 35-40 minutes.**

Cool.

Mix together and frost with:

1 cup powdered sugar
1 Tablespoon butter

1 Tablespoon cream
1 teaspoon almond extract

Sprinkle with sliced almonds or chopped pecans. Cut into 1 inch diagonal slices. May be topped with apple pie filling or sliced strawberries.

CANNOLI

A Little Old Italian Lady

14 Tablespoons sifted confectioners sugar
Fat for deep frying (½ olive oil and ½ vegetable shortening)
2 Tablespoons butter
1 egg
1 lb. Ricotta
1 cup sifted all-purpose flour
¼ lb. diced mixed candied fruits
3 Tablespoons cream sherry
1 teaspoon vanilla extract
1 Tablespoon wine vinegar
½ teaspoon ground cinnamon
1 Tablespoon heavy cream (or more)

Mix together: 2 tablespoons of the sugar, the butter, egg, flour, sherry, and vinegar. If too stiff, add a little water. Let dough stand at room temperature for about 30 minutes. Cut dough into pieces about the size of a walnut. Roll out each piece to an oval shape. Wrap each around an oiled wooden stick about 1 inch in diameter and 6 inches long. Seal the edges with a drop of cold water.

Heat the fat to 365 degrees on a frying thermometer. Gently remove the stick and drop each rolled wafer into the fat. Fry until golden brown. Lift out carefully. Drain and place on a cake rack to cool.

Drain the Ricotta. Be sure it is cold and dry, but not iced. Mix it with the remaining confectioners' sugar, the candied fruits, vanilla, cinnamon and cream. Mix well. Use to fill the cooled Cannoli. Refrigerate until ready to serve. Makes 12 Cannoli. *P

BROWNSTONE FRONT CAKE

(Richard's favorite cake)
Anna Marie Pizzitola Allen

1 cup shortening
2 ½ cups flour
2 ½ cups sugar
Pinch of salt
5 eggs
1 teaspoon vanilla
1 cup buttermilk
4 teaspoons cocoa
1 teaspoon baking soda

Cream shortening and sugar; add egg yolks. Put soda in buttermilk and add alternately with dry ingredients to creamed mixture. Add vanilla; fold in egg whites, after beating stiff. Bake in oblong pan (13x9x2) in a 350 degrees oven for 30-40 minutes.

Buttermilk Icing:

1 stick butter
½ cup milk
½ pint cream (coffee cream)
1 ¾ cup sugar

Cook over low heat until thick. *P

ITALIAN CREAM CAKE

Judy Grasso Peplinski (Bebe)

Cake	Icing
5 eggs	1 (8 oz. pkg) cream cheese
2 cups sugar	1 lb. box powdered sugar, sifted (about 4 cups)
1 stick oleo (soft)	1 stick (1/2 cup) oleo
½ cup shortening	1 teaspoon vanilla
1 cup buttermilk	chopped pecans
1 teaspoon vanilla	
2 cups flour, sifted	
¼ teaspoon salt	
1 teaspoon baking soda	
1 cup chopped pecans	
1 cup coconut	

Directions

Separate eggs. Beat whites until stiff. Cream sugar, oleo and shortening. Add yolks, one at a time, beating well after each. Add buttermilk alternately with flour, salt, baking soda. Add vanilla and fold in egg whites. Gently stir in pecans and coconut. Pour into three pans, (greased and floured). Bake in 350 degrees oven for 25-30 minutes. Cool 10 minutes, then remove from pans.

Icing

Beat all ingredients, except nuts. Mix well. Frost between layers, top and sides. Sprinkle top with chopped pecans.

TRACY'S SECRET BANANA BREAD

Tracy Peplinski

(Mary Anne's note: I save all my ripened bananas in my fridge drawer. They turn black and get squishy. But if there's no mildew—the riper, the better. I peel and smash them and get them to room temperature in the microwave. When I get 12 or so, I make three banana breads at a time. That's all my mixer bowl will hold. These are great with or without nuts and freeze very well.)

Preheat oven 350 degrees.

Sift together and set aside:

2 cups flour
1 teaspoon baking soda
¼ teaspoon salt

In mixer, cream together:

1 cup sugar
½ cup margarine, room-temperature (1 stick Parkay)
1 teaspoon vanilla

Add 2 eggs

Beat.

Smush ripened bananas with your hand (that's the Secret!).

Measure 1 ½ cups mashed bananas. Add mashed bananas alternately with dry ingredients to creamed mixture.

Add ½ cup chopped pecans (optional)

Bake in greased and floured bread pan in 350 degrees oven for 1 hour and 10 minutes.

BANANA NUT CAKE (JOHNNIE'S FAVORITE)

Mary Anne Scanlan Grasso

Cake

Sift together and set aside:
2 ½ cups flour
1 ½ teaspoons baking soda
1 ½ teaspoons baking powder
½ teaspoon salt

In mixer: Cream 1 and two-thirds cups sugar with two-thirds cup oleo (1 stick plus 2 Tablespoons. I prefer Parkay.)

Put 1 teaspoon vanilla in 1 cup buttermilk. Add to creamed mixture.

Mash and mix 1 cup of well-ripened bananas.

Alternate adding bananas and dry ingredients to creamed mixture.

Mix 2 minutes on slow speed. Add 2 whole eggs and beat 2 more minutes. Mix in one cup chopped pecans. Bake in 2 greased and floured 9-inch pans. Bake in 350 degrees oven about 25 minutes.

Test with toothpick.

Icing

1 box (about 4 cups) powdered sugar
1 pkg. cream cheese (8 ounces)
3 Tablespoons Parkay

About ½ mashed banana (a little at a time)

1 teaspoon vanilla

1 cup chopped pecans

Cream oleo and cream cheese in mixer and add the rest.

AUNT VERA FRENZA'S PINK STUFF

Beth Peplinski Triplett

(First, chill bowl and all ingredients, including cans.)

One recipe makes a BIG bowl full!

Blend 1 can Comstock Cherry Pie Filling with 1 can Eagle Brand condensed milk.

Add 1 can <u>well-drained</u> crushed pineapple (medium sized can)

Blend in 1 (12 oz.) carton Cool Whip.

Add 1 cup mini-marshmallows

*Optional: ½ cup pecans, chopped fine

(Refrigerating a day or two before serving is best.)

EASY RITZY COOKIES

Rachel Jill Peplinski Shamblin

Three ingredients are all you need:

Ritz crackers
Creamy peanut butter
White Almond Bark or Chocolate Chunks (or some of each)

Spread peanut butter on Ritz cracker. Place another Ritz on top. Set on wax paper.

After all cookies are made, break up candy and put it in a bowl.

Melt bark or chocolate in microwave oven for about 90 seconds. Stir lumps out.

Dip one cookie at a time with a fork into melted candy. Drain excess back into bowl. (Coat all sides good.)

Return to wax paper to dry. These are so good and no baking!

(Chocolate chips or Hershey's candy would work, too.)

GREEN STUFF

Taylor Renée Grasso

1 small box instant pistachio pudding
1 9 ounce container Cool Whip
1 20 ounce can crushed pineapple and juice
2 cups miniature marshmallows
1 cup finely chopped pecans, (optional)

Directions:

Chill bowl and pineapple.

Sprinkle dry pudding over Cool Whip in a large bowl.

Blend well. Add other ingredients and chill.

BEBE'S ICED CUT OUT SUGAR COOKIES

Judy Grasso Peplinski
(Julia Rose, 9-years-old, makes these.)
(Our family's favorite)

5 cups flour, sifted
2 ½ cups sugar
3 eggs
1 ½ cups real butter, softened—(3 sticks)
1 ¼ teaspoons baking powder
¾ teaspoons real vanilla
½ teaspoon salt

Sift dry ingredients. (Mix and set aside).

Cream butter and sugar in mixer.

Add eggs, one at a time, mixing well after each.

Add vanilla.

Gradually add dry ingredients.

Do not over beat.

Chill dough before cutting out so it is not sticky.

Use as little flour as possible.

Roll 1/3 inch thick.

Cut out with favorite cookie cutters.

Bake approx 10 minutes at 350 degrees in preheated oven.

Cool cookies on paper towels or cake racks.

ICING FOR CUT OUT COOKIES

4 ½ or 5 cups powdered sugar
1 stick real butter, softened
2 Tablespoons milk
1 teaspoon real vanilla

Mix above ingredients. Exact amount varies. Look at consistency and taste.

May need to add a little more powdered sugar and/or milk.

Tint with food coloring, if desired.

Ice cooled cookies and let them sit on wax paper for icing to get firm.

Best if stored in glass jar.

Stack cookies with wax paper in between them.

APPLESAUCE-BERRY GELATIN

Annette Silvio Highley

2 (3oz) packages strawberry gelatin
2 cups boiling water
1 can whole-berry cranberry sauce
1 ¾ cups <u>chunky</u> applesauce

Dissolve gelatin in boiling water. Stir in cranberry sauce and applesauce.

Pour into ring mold or bowl.

Cover and refrigerate overnight.

Delicious!

SPICED APPLE BUTTER

Jean Manning Scanlan

16 cups of thick apple pulp
8 cups sugar
1 cup white vinegar
4 teaspoons cinnamon

Peel and slice apples.

Add only enough water to cook. Cook with lid until soft.

Either press through a sieve or mash with a potato masher and measure.

Combine all ingredients in pot with apples.

Cook until mixture remains in a smooth mass when a little is cooled (About 1 ½ to 2 hours).

During cooking, stir frequently to prevent sticking and burning.

Pour into sterilized jars and seal while hot.

Makes 5 ½ quarts or 10 full pints.

AUNT BESSIE'S ORANGE FRUIT SALAD

Bessie Messina Frenza
Submitted by Bessie Marie Frenza Dycus

1 large carton cottage cheese
1 large box orange Jell-o
12 oz. carton Cool Whip
15 oz. can mandarin oranges
32 oz. can crushed pineapple

Drain fruit.

Mix everything and chill.

CHOCOLATE ÉCLAIRS

Rose Ann Scanlan Spudeck
(Can double recipe)

Bake 450 degrees oven for 15 minutes and 325 degrees oven for 15-20 minutes.

Melt 1 stick Parkay margarine in 1 cup of boiling water in pan on the stove.

Add 1 cup flour with ¼ teaspoon salt all at once. Cook slowly, stirring hard until mixture forms a ball that doesn't separate.

Remove from heat and cool slightly.

Add 4 whole eggs, one at a time, beating hard after each addition until mixture is smooth.

Grease cookie sheet. (I use Pam and wipe it out with a paper towel.)

Drop 2-3 inch long spoonfuls of dough about 2 inches apart on cookie sheet.

Don't mash them down! Makes about 12 or so.

Bake until puffed up and golden brown.

Cool on rack

Cut part way through one end.

Clean out any pulp inside.

Fill with vanilla pudding, closing up end.

Ice with chocolate icing or powdered sugar.

PUDDING FOR ÉCLAIRS

(My precious Mama's recipe for Banana Pudding)
Beulah Nell Scanlan

This recipe will fill a double batch of éclairs. (Or make a large banana pudding)

1 regular size can of Carnation milk
2 milk cans of water
3 large egg yolks
1 Tablespoon vanilla
1 ½ cups sugar
¾ cup flour (1/2 c. banana pudding)
½ teaspoon salt
(1 box Vanilla Wafers for Banana Pudding)

Sift flour, salt and sugar together. Use a whisk to mix really well. This will avoid lumpy pudding. Set aside. Separate eggs. (Put whites in fridge to keep cold for meringue when making Banana Pudding.)

In pot on the stove, add milk, water, egg yolks and vanilla, stirring constantly so it will not burn.

When milk mixture is almost to boiling point, slowly add dry ingredients. Continue to stir.

This pudding will thicken, but will not thicken as much as other puddings. That makes it less dry than other puddings!

(For Banana Pudding, layer pudding, Vanilla Wafers and sliced bananas. Top with No-Weep Meringue)

*See recipe for No-Weep Meringue for Banana Pudding and Cream Pies.

NO-WEEP MERINGUE

Aunt Ruth Frenza
(This is great for Banana Pudding or Cream Pies)

In a small saucepan, add: 2 Tablespoons sugar, 1 Tablespoon cornstarch, ½ cup water.

Cook, stirring constantly until clear and thick. Set aside.

In mixer, beat 3 chilled egg whites until soft and fluffy.

Add 6 Tablespoons sugar gradually, beating constantly.

Add 1/8 teaspoon salt and ½ teaspoon vanilla.

Add cornstarch mixture last. Beat until peaks stand. Don't overbeat.

Top banana pudding or cream pies with meringue.

Bake in hot oven 400-450 degrees until meringue is browned all over. This doesn't take long, so watch carefully!

*Do not make meringue and let it stand. Use immediately!

SWEET AUNT PATTI'S FRUIT COBBLER

Patricia Scanlan Ortega

1 stick real butter, melted
1 cup flour
2 ½ teaspoons baking powder
¾ cup milk

Mix all ingredients by hand. Not necessary to sift dry ingredients.

Pour into prepared pan or casserole dish.

Pour any type pie filling on top: apple, cherry, peach, etc. or a large can of crushed pineapple & juice.

Dough will rise up through fruit filling.

Bake in 350 degrees oven about 40 minutes or until golden brown.

Serve with whipped cream or ice cream.

*This recipe can be doubled or tripled, etc. for large group

SWEET AUNT PATTI'S STRAWBERRY CAKE

Patricia Scanlan Ortega

1 box white cake mix
2 Tablespoons flour
1 small box strawberry Jell-o
1 cup oil
½ cup water
4 eggs
½ cup of 10 oz. package frozen strawberries, sliced
(Patti puts a little more than ½ cup strawberries! Save ½ cup for frosting.)

Mix all ingredients together in mixer. Beat well.

Pour into big, heart-shaped cake pan that has been greased and floured.

Bake 25-35 minutes in 350 degrees oven.

See Strawberry Frosting Recipe below.

* How to make a heart-shaped cake.

Pour ½ batter into a 9-inch round cake pan and ½ batter into a 9-inch square pan.

Be sure the batter is evenly divided between pans so that when you put the layers together, they are the same height.

When cakes are completely cool (removing a hot cake from a pan can cause it to break into pieces), place the square cake on a large platter in a diamond position. Cut the round layer in half to make two half-circles. Carefully place the cut sides against the top sides of the "diamond." Voila!—a heart! –Heloise

STRAWBERRY CAKE FROSTING

Patricia Scanlan Ortega

1 box powdered sugar (approximately 4-5 cups)

4 Tablespoons real butter, melted

Add other ½ cup frozen strawberries—not so much juice

Mix well and spread on cake.

Makes a lot of frosting.

NONIE'S FRIED APPLE PIES

Beulah Nunn Scanlan

(I save old apples in my refrigerator drawer until I have a dozen or so. Or I buy a bag of Granny Smith apples. Even dried apples will work.)

Peel, core and cut up apples. Put them in a pot with a small amount of water. Bring to a boil and simmer with a lid until apples are done. Remove from heat. Mash them with a potato masher.

Add:

Sugar to sweeten to your taste. (My Mama said you can't put too much
   sugar or cinnamon).
2 teaspoons cinnamon
½ teaspoon ground allspice
¼ teaspoon ground cloves
Taste and adjust to your liking

(My precious Mama used to make her own biscuit dough from scratch. I buy canned biscuits! Some folks prefer pie crust and baking them in the oven. Nothing tastes as good as the way our mothers used to make them. Right?).

Roll out dough on floured surface and cut into a circle. Use a saucer to cut uniform circles. Put apple filling in center of circle. Fold over and crimp edges together with a fork dipped in flour. Lay pies on waxed paper until all are made. Fry in medium-hot oil in skillet. Drain on paper bag or paper towels. Enjoy!

AUNT ROSIE'S CHERRY CAKE— MOIST FRUITCAKE

Rosalie Grasso Macejewski

(This is one fruitcake you <u>won't</u> want to throw away!)

1 lb. dates, chopped

1 lb. pecans, chopped (Save some halves to decorate top of cake)

½ lb. candied cherries (¼ lb. red, ¼ lb. green), cut in halves or fourths.
   (Save some halves to decorate top of cake)

½ lb. candied pineapple, chopped

4 eggs

1 cup sugar

1 cup flour

1 teaspoon baking powder

¼ teaspoon salt

2 Tablespoons wine

Chop all fruit and nuts. Set nuts aside.

Add a little flour to fruit so it won't stick together. Set aside

Cream sugar and eggs together

Add baking powder, salt and wine to creamed mixture

Stir this into flour with a big spoon

Stir in fruit and nuts

Mix well

Spoon into tube pan greased with shortening. No flour. (I use a spring-type pan and cut a circle from a brown paper bag to fit in bottom of pan. I grease both pan and paper with shortening.)

Decorate top of cake with cherry halves and pecan halves

Bake in 325 degrees oven for one hour

Remove from pan while still warm. Cool fruitcake completely before wrapping it.

Wrap fruitcake with cheesecloth or a white cloth soaked with wine. (I prefer Mogan David Blackberry wine)

Make fruitcake at least a couple weeks or longer before eating it for best results.

Store in airtight container until ready to use. Keep cloth moist with wine.

PECAN SANDIES

Rose Ragusa

2 cups butter or margarine
1 cup powdered sugar
4 teaspoons vanilla
2 cups flour
2 Tablespoons of water
½ cup chopped pecans

Preheat oven to 300 degrees. Beat butter and sugar till fluffy. Beat in vanilla and 2 tablespoons water. Reduce speed; add flour. Stir in pecans. Shape dough into 1 inch balls. Place on ungreased baking sheet. Flatten with finger. **Bake 20 to 25 minutes.** Cool on racks. Sprinkle with powdered sugar.

NONIE'S OLD FASHIONED TEA CAKES

Beulah Nunn Scanlan

(This recipe has been in our family for over 250 years!)

9 cups flour

3 cups sugar

1 teaspoon salt

¾ cup shortening, room temperature

2 teaspoons baking powder

4 whole eggs

½ teaspoon baking soda

No vanilla or other flavoring

1 *heaping* teaspoon nutmeg

2 *heaping* teaspoons cinnamon

Sift dry ingredients in a very large container. (I use my big roaster pan.)

Cream sugar, shortening and eggs in mixer.

Add creamed mixture with dry ingredients.

Do not mix or handle dough more than necessary or it will be tough.

Roll out dough to at least ¼ inch thick on lightly floured surface.

Cut out cookies with a large cookie cutter (a tuna can or wide-mouth jar lid works best).

Bake on lightly greased cookie sheet or parchment paper.

Bake at 375 degrees about 10-11 minutes or until bottoms are lightly browned. Tops are white.

Store in glass jar with tight lid. Great to dunk in coffee or cold milk!

AUNT ROSE ANN'S DARK, MOIST CHOCOLATE CAKE

Rose Ann Scanlan Spudeck
(Our family's favorite for all occasions)

Preheat oven to 350 degrees.

Grease and flour an oblong pan or three round pans. Set aside.

Sift together:

2 ¼ cups flour
¾ cup cocoa
2 teaspoons baking soda
½ teaspoon salt

Blend in mixer:

2 cups sugar
1 cup oil

Add:

2 whole eggs
1 cup buttermilk with 2 teaspoons vanilla mixed in.

Blend a little, then add dry ingredients to creamed mixture. Add 1 cup of boiling water last and beat on medium speed for two minutes. Pour into prepared pans. **Bake at 350 degrees** for about 25 minutes for round pans and 35-40 minutes for oblong pan. Cake freezes well. This cake is delicious plain or with your favorite frosting. We like Snow Peak Icing on it.

AUNT RUTH'S SNOW PEAK ICING

Ruth Jensen Frenza

In mixer, beat 2 egg whites until form peaks.

Add ¼ teaspoon salt.

At the same time, put 1 ¼ cups white Karo syrup in a pot.

Bring syrup just to a good rolling boil.

Pour gradually into egg whites, beating all the while.

Add 2 teaspoons vanilla.

Beat until soft peaks form.

Do not overbeat or will dry out!

Makes a lot of icing.

Delicious!

BISCOTTI

Frances De Francesco

4 whole eggs
2 egg yolks
1 cup of sugar
1 teaspoon Anise flavoring
1 ½ cups of flour
¾ cup chopped, roasted Filberts
½ cup candied cherry halves
½ cup butter
2 cups of flour sifted with 4 teaspoons baking powder

Baking Time: 25 minutes

Oven Temperature: 350 degrees

Browning Time: 15 minutes

Yield 30 slices or more

Beat the eggs with the 2 yolks in a bowl. Add the sugar and flavoring. Sift the first amount of flour into the mixture. Add the coarsely chopped roasted filberts and the cherry halves.

Add the softened butter, and last, the flour sifted with the baking powder; mixing well.

Form the dough into 4 long loaves upon a buttered and floured pan using a wooden spoon.

Bake in a moderate oven until firm. Remove from the oven and cut each loaf into ½ inch slices. Replace slices in the pan and bake to a golden brown.

RECIPE FOR A GOOD MARRIAGE

Source Unknown

3 cups full of Love
4 spoons full of Hope
2 cups full of Warmth
2 spoons full of Tenderness
1 cup of Forgiveness
1 pint of Faith
1 cup of Friends
1 barrel of Laughter

Combine Love and Warmth. Mix thoroughly with Tenderness.

Add Forgiveness and blend with Friends and Hope.

Sprinkle in Good Times together.

Stir in a generous amount of Faith and Laughter.

Bake with Sunshine.

Say God's blessings over it and serve daily in generous helpings.

TIMELESS TRADITIONS

Tradition. What a lovely, meaningful word. Just saying it out loud—tradition—evokes marvelous images in one's memory bank. Many of us value certain time-honored customs and practices that have been passed down to us from our loved ones. Perhaps for generations. One such time-honored tradition is the Saint Joseph Table. Some refer to it as the Saint Joseph Altar. Most Catholics recognize Saint Joseph as the faithful, caring husband of Mary, the Blessed Mother, and the devoted earthly father of Jesus, the Christ. But many are unaware that he has a special feast day—March 19th—just two days after the celebrated Saint Patrick's Day. This lesser known feast day celebration honors Saint Joseph, among other things, for answered prayers. Answered prayers today as well as those that date back to The Middle Ages.

The story begins over 500 years ago in Sicily. An exceptionally severe famine struck the land. No rain fell for an extended period of time. No vegetables or fruit or grain would grow with the exception of the fava bean. Many people starved to death. Sorrow filled every home. Everyone prayed to God to end the drought. They also prayed to San Giuseppe (Saint Joseph), their patron saint, to intercede with God to send them rain. They promised that if their prayers were answered they would have a special feast honoring God and San Giuseppe.

A miracle! The rains came—bringing abundant crops. The people rejoiced! They kept their promise. Since food was their greatest possession, everyone prepared a feast of foods from their bountiful harvests in thanksgiving. A huge table displayed their fruits and vegetables, with special baked breads and sweets. Fish and pasta took the place of meat, which was a scarcity. This became known as a "meatless feast". The priest came and blessed the food. Then, *all* were invited to partake of the celebration—friends and strangers alike. Even the poorest of the poor shared in the bounty. Everyone gave thanks and praise to God for His gracious blessings. This festivity has become known as Tavola di San Giuseppe—Table of Saint Joseph.

In 1870, Pope Pius IX proclaimed Joseph as the Patron of the universal Church, honoring his role of support, protection and guidance and named March 19 as "the {heavenly} birthday of St. Joseph". Pius XII added a second feast of Joseph the Worker, which is celebrated May 1st, the traditional Labor Day.

Now, unlike Saint Patrick's Day, usually no parade or exuberant public celebrations mark Saint Joseph's Day. However, around the world, in homes, churches and organizations, simple and elaborate feasts are being lovingly prepared---sometimes weeks ahead of time—by the hard-working faithful. They petition and offer thanks to Saint Joseph for his kindnesses and intercessions on their behalf and on the behalf of others.

Over the years, reasons to offer the Altar have varied: the safe return of a loved one from the war, for healing of the sick, to mend broken relationships, to fulfill a promise, in thanksgiving for answered prayer, and so on. The favor requested must never be for personal gain or benefit.

Begging (Questua) has to be a humbling experience. Asking for food items or donations for an Altar has been passed on from one generation to another. This tradition honors the Saint whose feast day is celebrated.

Asking for others and not for oneself possibly helps to make the begging easier.

Perhaps the most unusual item on the Altar is the lucky fava bean. "The gift of a blessed bean is the most well known of the customs associated with the St. Joseph's Day Altar. During one of Sicily's severe famines, the fava bean thrived while other crops failed. It was originally grown for animal fodder, but because of its amazing resilience, it became sustaining food for the farmers and their families. The dried bean is commonly called the "lucky bean." Legend has it that the person who carries a 'lucky bean' will never be without coins. The fava bean is a token of the St. Joseph's Altar, and a reminder to pray to St. Joseph, particularly for the needs of others." (Gretna:1998)

The shape of the Altar is in that of a cross. Three tiers in the center of the Altar symbolize The Holy Trinity. A table on either side completes the cross. White linens cover these structures. Often, netting and ribbon decorate the tables. A statue or picture of Saint Joseph, often holding Baby Jesus and a lily, is usually centered on the top tier. The Altar is an amazingly beautiful work of art. Vibrant colors everywhere: fresh flowers, fresh fruits and fresh vegetables, candles, wine bottles, holy pictures and small religious statues, huge, round loaves of braided bread, inedible bread sculptures depicting religious meaningful symbols: sandals, chalices, monstrances, ladders and saws, hammers and nails, fish, cross, etc. (See Glossary.) All sorts of homemade cakes, cookies etc. adorn the Altar. Many hands and many hours of loving, dedicated work have gone into the creation of such beauty.

Often, one large, whole, baked fish adorns the Altar symbolizing Christ and Christianity. Sometimes it's depicted in a highly decorative cake shaped like a large fish with scales and fins.

Other artistically decorated cakes in the shape of The Holy Bible or a Lamb of God cake can be seen. Every available space on the Altar is filled with something meaningful to this feast day.

Saint Joseph's feast day is a family affair. One of the traditions is to have young children portray Jesus, Mary and Joseph and other favored saints, sometimes in costumes, at a special table. At one time, the custom was to have twelve "saints", but today it varies in number. Another custom passed down is to serve each "saint" a small portion of certain foods from the Altar after the Altar and all its foods have been blessed by a priest. It is customary for the "saints" to eat everything served to them.

One of the more popular and integral Altar traditions is "Tupa, Tupa"— "Knock, Knock". Three "saints" portraying Jesus, Mary and Joseph knock on three doors seeking shelter, signifying the night of Jesus' birth. "The ritual begins with St. Joseph knocking on three doors. At the first two doors, people inside ask, "Who is there?" The response is, "Jesus, Mary and Joseph." "What do you want?" They ask. The response, "We seek food and shelter." They are told "There is no room for you here." When the Holy Family arrives at the third door, (where the Altar is), St. Joseph says, "We seek food and shelter." The joyful response is, "Welcome to this house! The table is set. The food is prepared. Come in and honor us with your presence!"

(Source: 21st Annual St. Joseph's Altar-Sacred Heart Society of Little York March 15th 2009)

Today, at the Altar served to the public in churches or organizations, it is also the custom to serve a "meatless" pasta dinner, usually with hard boiled eggs served with the wonderfully seasoned sauce, along with some cooked green vegetable, a tossed salad, bread, drink and dessert. Special, seasoned breadcrumbs, "Mudica/Mudrica/Mollica— symbolizing sawdust, is offered to those who like to top their pasta and sauce (Suga) with it. There can be a set fee or donation basket for the meal. All proceeds are spent on the needy. This demonstration of selflessness and charity is the most important tradition of the Saint Joseph's Altar that can be handed down to our children, grandchildren and greats for generations to come.

"Whether a St. Joseph Altar is an elaborate display at an elegant church or a humble table in a modest home, it is a reflection of deep devotion to St. Joseph, the patron of those in need—workers, travelers, the persecuted, the poor, the aged, the dying. And it is a custom that has enjoyed resurgence in recent years, as young and old have begun to rediscover their heritage. After many centuries, the St. Joseph Altar still serves as a reminder that those who have enjoyed some measure of good fortune must share it with those who have less."

Activity Source: *Viva San Giuseppe* by St. Joseph Guild, St. Joseph Guild, 1200 Mirabeau Ave. New Orleans, Louisiana 70122

THE ALTAR CUSTOMS
AND SYMBOLS

Assumption Catholic Church brochure/ March 2009

There is a symbolism in everything that is placed on the Altar. Below are many examples of that symbolism:

Altar	Constructed in three tiers representing the THREE persons in the Holy Trinity.
Angels	Angels with trumpets announcing Christ's coming.
Bible	Large cake decorated to look like a Bible
Bread of St. Joseph	A specially prepared bread is blessed and then distributed at the altar.
Breadcrumbs (Mudica)	Browned and seasoned bread crumbs sprinkled over the pasta, representing the sawdust of Joseph, the carpenter.
Burro (donkey)	The transportation of Joseph, Mary and Jesus.
Butterflies	New Life
Citrus Fruits (Oranges/Lemons)	Abundance of the Earth.
Cross	Crucifixion of Christ

Cuccidatti	These large breads are decorated with cookies, candies and special figs intricately shaped and sculpted into beautiful, meaningful symbols.
Cupid	Holy Spirit
Dove	The Holy Spirit
Fava Bean	The gift of a blessed bean is the most well-known of the customs associated with the Altar. During one of Sicily's severe famines, the fava bean thrived while other crops failed. Legend has it that the person who carries a "lucky bean" will never be without coins. The fava bean also is a token of the St. Joseph's Altar, and a reminder to pray to St. Joseph.
Fig Leaves	Represent the fig orchards of Sicily and the dried figs used to make the cuccidatti.
Fish	Christian symbol of Jesus and Christianity
Grapes	Vineyards of Sicily
Hammer, Nails, Pliers, Saw	The tools of trade that St. Joseph used as a carpenter.
Heart	The Sacred Heart of Jesus and the Immaculate Heart of Mary
Lamb Cake	Jesus, the Lamb of God
Lemons	The Orchards of Italy
Lilies	Purity and Humility
Monstrance	Holds the Sacred Host
Palm	The Palms waved on Jesus' path into Jerusalem
Panne Grosso (Big Bread)	Devotional breads are wreath-shaped and each represents the saints.
Pea Pod	Abundance of the Earth.
Peacocks	Eternity

Pignolatti	Fried pastry molded in the shape of pine cones representing the pine cones that Jesus played with as a child.
Pineapple	Hospitality
Pupaculova	Baked bread filled with dyed Easter eggs symbolizing the coming of Easter.
Rooster	Proclaiming the news about Jesus' birth.
Roses	Blessed Mother Mary
Sandals	Represent the feet of Jesus, Mary and Joseph.
Sheaves of Wheat	Abundance of the Earth
Staff	St. Joseph's Staff
Star	The Star of Bethlehem
Sun, Moon and Stars	Led the Magi to Bethlehem to see Baby Jesus.
Wine	The Miracle at Cana and The Blood of Our Savior.
Wreath	The Crown of Thorns

BIBLIOGRAPHY

Alborghetti, Marci. *The American Prayer Book: In God We Trust.* New Jersey: The Catholic Book Publishing Corp. 2012. Print.

A Prayer to St. Joseph, the Worker, from Pope Pius IX. Bulin.com. 19 Mar. 2004. Web. <http://www.bulin.com/stjoe/sjprayer.html>.

A Ritual Prayer to St. Joseph in Sicilian Initaly.com. 04 Feb. 2003. Web. <http://www.initaly.com/regions/sicily/joetabl.htm>.

"Blessed Josemaria Escriva." *Bulin.com.* 19 Mar. 2004. Web. <http://www.bulin.com/stjoesjprayer.html>.

"Catholic Traditions." *Wikipedia.org.* Web. <http://en.wikipedia.org/wiki/SaintJoseph'sDay>.

Champlin, Msgr. Joseph, and Msgr. Kenneth Lasch. *Day by Day with St. Joseph.* New Jersey: The Catholic Book Publishing Corp. 2010. Print.

Chupa, Anna, Field notes. *"Fava Bean."* *Erc.msstate.edu.* 18 Mar. 1998. Web. <http://www.erc.msstate.edu/-achupa/STJO/sj_stand.html>.

Delaney, John J. *Dictionary of Saints*, The 2nd ed. Doubleday, a Division of Random House, 1980. Print.

Echoes St. Joseph—"The Silent Saint" Dominican Nuns Farmington Hills, MI Spring 2013 Vol 58 No 1. Print.

"Fava Beans." *Fisheaters.com*. 14 May 2007. Web. <http://www.fisheaters.com/customslent5.html>.

Filas, F. L. "St. Joseph." *The New Catholic Encyclopedia Devotions to St. Joseph*: Milwaukee. 1944. Print.

Heloise. "Hints From Heloise." *Houston Chronicle* [Houston] Feb. 2012, D-Movies sec. Print.

"Inedible Dough." *Italiansrus.com*. 14 May 2007. Web. <http://www.italiansrus.com/articles/stjosephsymbols.htm>.

Ladies of the Sacred Heart Cookbook. Lenexa: Cookbook, 2010. Print.

Pizzitola Family Cookbook. *Pizzitola Family Cookbook III*. Lenexa: Cookbook, 1997. Print.

Pope Pius IX proclaimed Joseph as Patron of the Universal Church and March 19th as "the {heavenly} birthday of St. Joseph". *Bulin.com*. Franciscan Mission Associates. 19 Mar. 2004. Web. <http://www.bulin.com/stjoe/sjprayer.html>.

Prayer to St. Joseph *Bulin.com*. Catholic Online. 19 Mar.2004. Web. <http://bulin.com./stjoe/sjprayer.html>.

St. Bernadine of Siena. "Sermon 2, On Joseph." *Fisheaters.com*. 14 May 2007. Web. <http://www.fisheaters.com/customslent5.html>.

"St. Joseph Bread-Pane di San Giuseppe." *Recipelink.com*. The Kitchen Link, Inc., 1995-2012. Web. <http://www.recipelink.com>.

St. Joseph's Altar. 1946. Photograph. Houston Chronicle, Houston. Print.

Souvay, Charles L. "St. Joseph". Catholic.com. 2008. Web. http://oce.catholic.com/index.php?title=Joseph%2CSaint.

The Altar Customs and Symbols. Houston: Assumption Catholic Church. 2009. Brochure. Print.

To St. Joseph for Protection. *Bulin.com.* Franciscan Mission Association. 19Mar.2004. Web <http:wwwbulin.com/stjoe/sjprayer.html>.

The New American Bible. **St. Joseph ed.** New York: Catholic Book Publishing. 1970. Print.

Viva San Giuseppe. New Orleans: St. Joseph Guild. Brochure from St. Ignatius Loyola Church. Spring, Texas. Print.

"We Come to Your Feast" Words and Music. Text and Tune Michael Joncas b.1951 copyright 1994 GIA Publications, Inc. Print.

www.wikianswers.com Distance from Bethlehem to Egypt

www.arewethereyet.com Distance from Egypt to Nazareth

www.google.com Distance from Jerusalem to Bethlehem

www.wikianswers.com Distance from Nazareth to Bethlehem